ELLIOTT'S
SPORTS
ANALYSIS
SECRETS

This book is dedicated to my Grandson
born on 9th November 2014

WILLIAM KAY ELLIOTT

ELLIOTT'S SPORTS ANALYSIS SECRETS

KEITH ELLIOTT

RACING POST

Published in 2015 by Raceform
Compton, Newbury, Berkshire, RG20 6NL

Copyright ©Keith Elliott 2015

The right of Keith Elliott to be identified as the author of this work has
been asserted by him in accordance with the Copyright, Designs and
Patents Act 1988.

A catalogue record for this book is available from the British Library.

ISBN: 978-1-910498-15-6
EBOOK: 978-1-910498-17-0

Designed by Fiona Pike

Printed and bound in the UK by CPI Group (UK) Ltd, Croydon, CR0 4YY

CONTENTS

ABOUT THE AUTHOR

'The thinking man's pundit' — *Sunday Times*

Keith Elliott has run sports betting services ever since he operated what was probably the country's first in 1992. His vast sporting knowledge, shrewd analytical research and quality contacts, together with his insights into personal motivation, make him a legendary name in sports betting.

His original analytical approach to sports betting prompted the *Sunday Times* to call Keith, 'the thinking man's pundit'.

He has written countless articles and books, notably 13 annual editions of the acclaimed and award winning *Elliott's Golf Form*, known as the 'Golf punter's Bible', and *'How To Win At Golf Betting'*. He was also a weekly columnist for *The Sportsman* newspaper.

His varied career in broadcasting began in 1978 when he became BBC Radio Merseyside's Racing Correspondent, a position he held for over 18 years until in 1997 he became a government appointed director of the Horserace Betting Levy Board. Throughout his nine years of service Keith worked tirelessly on behalf of punters and was quickly dubbed 'The Punters' Champion' as he built a reputation as a passionate supporter of both punters and racegoers.

His television career includes regular appearances as an analyst on the At the Races programme 'Fill Yer Boots' and on The Sportsxchange.

In September 2013, after over 20 years of running successful sports betting services for other companies, he launched his own website, elliottsportsanalysis.co.uk.

NEW!
ELLIOTT'S SPORTS ANALYSIS SERVICE

To coincide with writing this book Keith on Sept 1st 2014 started an exciting NEW sports service which focuses on Golf and Football.

HOW MUCH WILL IT COST?
Less than 99p per day. The fee is £29 per month, £78 for three months, £150 for 6 months, or £275 for 12 months.

WHAT WILL I RECEIVE AS A MEMBER?
Monday
The Monday High Noon Round Up [MHNRU]
The MHNRU analyses the previous week's two transatlantic golf tournaments highlighting players who are potential winners, 'bottlers' to oppose, and 'name' players who are improving or on the decline. There will also be reflective analysis on the weekend's key PL matches.

Tuesday
The outright Golf line
Outright bets for the week's European Tour and USPGA tournaments. Two minimal stake EW Transatlantic doubles.

Wednesday
The non-outright golf bet line
One, maybe two, non-outright golf bets from nationality, top 10, top 20, or R1 leader markets.

Friday
The Friday 5pm football line.
This line will give the best bets for three PL w/end matches. This line shows profits to rec. stakes pre Xmas of over 26 points.

Sunday
The Sunday Supplement line for all golf's WGCs + Majors.
On the final morning of all the WGCs and Majors Keith will use his unique database of players' records when in contention to give both his best outright bet and his best R4 two ball bets.

Ante post bets will be given mainly for golf and football, and occasionally for other sports. With a General Election on May 7th 2015 Keith, who gave David Cameron at 16/1 to be the next Conservative leader, will include his analysis and best bets as part of the service.

HOW DO I JOIN?

Simply go to elliottsportsanalysis.co.uk and join at once.

GOLF RESULTS – GOLF MAJORS AND WGCS

Keith has given 8 winners in the 9 Majors and 9 WGCs since August 2012 incl. four of the last six majors.

Total profits to rec.stakes has been 258 points — usual stake 12 pts per event.

2014

USPGA — R. McIlroy W 5/1
US Open — M. Kaymer W 40/1
WGC/Matchplay — J Day W 20/1

2013

USPGA — J Dufner W 40/1
The Open — P Mickelson W 22/1
WGC/Matchplay — M Kuchar W 28/1

2012

WGC/HSBC — I Poulter W 20/1
USPGA — R McIlroy W 20/1

"I have been a member of Keith's service for some 15 years and can't remember ever being disappointed with each year's results. Keith is so much more than a tipster he is a Sports Analyst who explains the logic of his decisions using techniques that are beyond the reach of ordinary punters like myself."

TR Surrey.

Shamrock Express

IRISH HORSE RACING SPECIALIST

'GET ON BOARD' and start backing Irish Racing with CONFIDENCE

Our service is NOT a form-based tipping service.
We bring you top INFO from the Irish scene.

Below are just some of our limited advised Antepost bets that have
been sent as part of the membership fee over the years :

QUEVEGA @ 4/1 (Mares Hurdle 2009) W @ 2/1 advised in Jan 09

CHAMPAGNE FEVER @ 25/1 (Champion Bumper 2012) W @ 16/1 advised December 2011

VAUTOUR @ 10/1 (Supreme Novices 2014) W @ 7/2 advised Dec 2013

STUCCODOR @ 9/1 (Irish Lincoln) W @ 11/2

AUSTRALIA @ 25/1 (Epsom Derby 2014) advised June 2013 W @ 11/8

THOMAS EDISON @ 6/1 (Galway Hurdle 2014) W @ 7/2

There are NO Monthly Fees, No Crazy Membership Costs
and No Premium Phone Rates.

For a small joining fee you receive various FREE INFO and then only
'PAY AS YOU WIN' on our advised MAX bets.

For full details and how to 'GET ON BOARD' visit our website

www.shamrockexpress.co.uk

For many years we operated under the Goldcall banner
and achieved great profits for their members.

We have packages to suit all pockets starting at £40 for a season.

(All bets proofed to Racing Post)

FOREWORD

In the mid-1990s I would bet on football but not golf. How on earth could you pick a player out from a field of 156 with any confidence? Betting on golf seemed to be total guesswork! Then, one day in 1994 in my new job at William Hill I picked up a copy of 'Elliott's Golf Form' and my eyes were opened by Keith's first book.

I'd just graduated from Leeds with a psychology degree so I liked 'thinky stuff ' and this was eye opening! The confusion of past results started to be unraveled by no end of stimulating reasoning as Keith introduced concepts such as The Nappy Factor, Mental Let Down, Inspiration by Comparison, and The Comeback Trail to explain why winning golfers had enjoyed a crucial, but not immediately obvious, edge.

By sheer chance, the man who interviewed me for the William Hill job, Mike Grenham, had done the exact same psychology degree several years earlier so he too was intrigued by Keith's writings. With his book our 'Bible', Mike and I set up a weekly golf betting syndicate and the profits started to roll in so it was a really sad day when the book's run ended after thirteen editions in 2007.

So I was naturally thrilled when Keith got in touch in 2014 to tell me that he was to write a new book, *Elliott's Sports Analysis Secrets* on the 20th anniversary of his first.

In this new book, Keith's ever-enquiring mind has re-visited all his original concepts, developed them in greater detail, introduced new ones such as 'The God Squad and The Gay Factor!' and taken the logical and exciting step of applying them to a range of sports.

Football features heavily in 'Sports Analysis Secrets' with plenty of examples from the recent World Cup in Brazil. One particularly fascinating case study is Luis Suarez. Seemingly desperate to get away from Anfield during the summer of 2013 as he served a lengthy ban Liverpool fans feared the worst. However, as you'll read, watching Suarez produce the season of his life and pick up award after award came as no surprise to Keith as the Uruguayan had several big motivational factors working in his favour.

Keith's fresh eye also gives us new explanations for shocks from Australia's 5-0 whitewash of England in the last Ashes series to Kenny Dalglish's surprise resignation from Liverpool in 1991.There are also fresh interesting new examples of Keith's best known and compelling concept, The Nappy Factor, which he has now amended and redefined.

The expansion of the concept of 'Mental Let Down' now enables it to be applied to short-term events such as teams conceding a goal just after they have scored and I was fascinated to learn how celebrating a goal can lead to defeat and death! The MLD concept can also be applied to season-long struggles such as Manchester United's poor campaign after the departure of Sir Alex Ferguson. The bad news for me as a Liverpool fan is that combining The Comeback Trail — Keith has applied it to teams as well as to individuals — with 'Mental Let Down' suggests conditions are now ripe for Manchester United to restore their traditional dominance over Liverpool in the Premier League.

Anyone who likes a bet or is just interested in how we humans operate will be captivated from first page to last when they read 'Elliott's Sports Analysis Secrets'. In fact, I'd go as far as saying that your pre- or post-match discussions will never be the same again!

Dave Tindall
Golf analyst for Rotoworld

INTRODUCTION

WHY HAVE I WRITTEN THIS BOOK?

Last year it was exactly 20 years since the first Elliott's Golf Form book was published. In the subsequent 13 annuals many concepts and ideas were introduced and applied to golf. So 20 years on all these concepts have been developed and applied to other sports as well as to golf. There are also two new factors with an assessment of how religious belief, and the 'coming out' of gay sportsmen and women may affect sporting performance.

WHY THE REFERENCE TO 'SECRETS' IN THE BOOK'S TITLE?

One of the concepts I created was The Nappy Factor which the great golf writer Peter Dobereiner writing in Golf World called the 'New secret of golf betting'. As well as The Nappy Factor I had also created six other important factors that could, to use Dobereiner's term, be called 'secrets' so 'Sports Analysis Secrets' seemed to be an appropriate title.

So as well as The Nappy Factor therefore we will also be returning to examine, develop and update all those other six factors which are

- The importance of Landmark birthdays
- The Funeral Factor
- Inspiration by Comparison [IBC]
- Mental Let Down [MLD]
- The Comeback Trail [CT]
- Positive and Negative Mental Associations [PMAs and NMAs]

And there will also be two new additional chapters

- The God Squad and The Gay Factor which examine whether religious belief and 'coming out' affect sports performance.

We all know that in sports analysis there are always certain factors that must be taken into account such as recent form, injury news, the weather, and any change of coach or manager. **However, in this book as you can see above we'll examine only the other less obvious factors that can be so important in providing extra hidden motivation.** 'You see what you look for' is one of life's great truisms so once you understand these factors you'll be amazed how often you will see them at work.

USING THE BOOK AS A SPORTS BETTING PUNTER

There are really two issues here. The first is accessing the relevant information, and the second is using it profitably.

ACCESSING INFORMATION

Today with the social media, daily tweets from sportsmen, 24 hour TV

Sports channels plus Wikipedia there is plenty of material out there. Obtaining information re injuries, operations and general health as well as details of weddings, pregnancies, babies and family bereavements are a matter of keeping as up to date as possible by accessing as many news sources as you can. The simple fact is that today, more than any other time in our sporting history, there is more access to more relevant information than ever before.

USING THE 'SECRETS' AS BETTING TOOLS.

The individual concepts do not in themselves act directly as pointers to specific selections. They are indicators that a particular individual or team is likely to play above or below their recent level of form and so take a step forward or backward in their personal career or team position.

Let's make a comparison with Timeform the famous racing form service that gives symbols to racehorses. For example the P symbol suggests that the horse will show significant improvement. However, in its next race it may not be a selection because its stable may be out of form, the going may be unsuitable, or it has too much weight.

Let's be clear the 'secrets' can be the basis for successful sports betting as we know from Dave Tindall in his Foreword. Indeed he and Mike Grenham, both honours psychology graduates, set up a highly profitable syndicate applying the 'secrets' to golf.

It worked because, in Dave's own words, 'The confusion of past results started to be unraveled by no end of stimulating reasoning as concepts such as The Nappy Factor, Mental Let Down, Inspiration by Comparison, and The Comeback Trail explained why winning golfers had enjoyed a crucial, but not immediately obvious edge'.

Finally, please note that throughout the book a series of real life examples will be used. In most cases the conclusions can be applied to both male and female athletes but it would make for extremely tedious reading to continuously repeat the point **so please note that 'sportsman' should be read as shorthand for 'sportsman AND sportswoman'.**

The book is divided into FOUR sections

SECTION ONE
CHAPTER ONE — The importance of mental skills

Here we examine the growth in the importance of mental skills in sport with TEN recent examples taken from SIX different sports involving the use of FIVE different mental skills gurus including England taking Dr Steve Peters and his 'Inner Chimp' to the World Cup.

The significance for individuals and teams who start using a sports psychologist for the first time is also examined.

SECTION TWO

In this section we look at three key life events — **births, birthdays and deaths** — that so often cause sportsmen to re-view, re-evaluate, and re-examine their sporting lives in ways that can often lead to greater motivation and so improved results.

CHAPTER TWO — The Nappy Factor

The Nappy Factor concept — which originally applied to first time fathers — is developed here to include the impact before the birth and the positive effect if the second child is the first son. There are also EIGHT recent examples covering FOUR different sports of this wider definition of The Nappy Factor.

CHAPTER THREE — The importance of Landmark birthdays

Here we first consider with examples the importance of the Nines when at 29, 39 and even 49 sportsmen often re-examine their lives and so as a result often make 'big' and possibly regrettable decisions. We then move on to discuss with examples how the passing of key Landmark birthdays at 30, 40 and even 50 can stimulate improved sporting performance.

CHAPTER FOUR — The Funeral Factor

This concept was originally used to show how immediately after a bereavement an individual or team could be inspired to a higher level of performance. Here we extend its scope to include the effect of 'near death' experiences, the impact that can **precede** a bereavement, and the way in which the death of a loved one can have an impact many years later. The examples cover FIVE sports including the Golf major in which both the winner and runner-up were inspired by The Funeral Factor, as well as unusual examples in 2014 from the World Cup, a Division One football match and a Test match in Australia.

SECTION THREE

In this section we examine two NEW factors to see if they improve sporting performance.

CHAPTER FIVE — The God Squad

Here we assess to what extent deeply held religious belief can improve sporting performance.

CHAPTER SIX — The Gay factor

The question here is to what extent if at all does 'coming out' as a gay sportsman lead to improved sporting performance.

SECTION FOUR

In this section we return to consider the other concepts that affect sporting performance that I first created 20 years ago.

CHAPTER SEVEN — Inspiration by Comparison [IBC]

For the first time IBC is divided into FIVE key categories covering a total of TWENTY THREE examples including FOURTEEN examples from the last two years. There is also the golfer who used IBC in two different ways on his way to becoming the World's No 1, and how a former alcoholic golfer inspired another ex-alcoholic golfer to golfing success.

CHAPTER EIGHT — Mental Let Down [MLD]

Originally MLD referred solely to the difficulty a golfer has in trying to follow one win with another the next week. So originally I was using MLD only after a tournament and only in relation to golf.

However, here it becomes a powerful, dynamic, versatile multi-use term as the MLD concept is extended to include its impact not just after but **within** a tournament or match, after a successful **season**, and also after **failure**. It is also applied to four sports other than golf. This chapter also refers to The Law of the Streaker, The Cyclops Factor, and how scoring a goal can lead to defeat and death!

CHAPTER NINE — The Comeback Trail [CT]

Introduced in my first book it referred to the extra motivation a golfer has when on the CT after injury. Here the concept is developed by referring to the FOUR different time periods before a comeback can be achieved, and to the EIGHT possible background reasons that can cause a player to be on the CT. There are also TWELVE examples from the last two years of successful CT sportsmen drawn from FIVE different sports, before finally the CT is applied to team sports.

CHAPTER TEN — Positive and Negative Mental Associations [PMAs and NMAs]

PMAs are illustrated by NINE examples involving THREE different sports before we reverse PMAs and see how powerful NMAs can be.

AUTHOR'S NOTE

This book includes examples drawn from and references to FOURTEEN different sports up to Xmas Day 2014.

CHAPTER ONE
THE IMPORTANCE
OF MENTAL SKILLS

One day 'out of the blue' in 1993 at Haydock Park racecourse I was asked if I would write a Golf Form Book. After all I was told that there was a Form Book for horse racing with all the racing results in so why not have a Golf Form book with results for all the tournaments on the European and American tours. I supposed I was asked as I included golf in a sport betting service that I was then operating. However, there was no way I was simply going to produce just a list of results as I realised that the book gave me the opportunity to include all aspects of Golf Betting especially my passionate belief that Golf was essentially a mental, not just a technical game, and so I could draw on my interest in personal motivation.

I'd given many presentations and addressed many audiences from small seminars to a London theatre full of BT employees on the subject of personal motivation for many, many years. The more I'd studied and presented such material the more convinced I became of its importance. The feedback was always very good, I knew for certain that it had helped many people. I also knew that it had certainly helped me and I'd received, and still cherish, the many letters I received as a result of those presentations.

So then with the opportunity to write a Golf Form book I had the chance to fully apply my mental skills work to professional golf. After all Golf is essentially a mental game because in a round of golf lasting over 4 hours at least half of the time you don't actually play so in that time the golfer is thinking and 'talking to himself', with the danger that with Golf being so tough and demanding this self-talk would inevitably include 'negative' thoughts that would adversely affect performance.

So rather than simply list scores and results I decided to relate mental skills to golf, golf performance and golf betting, and although golf was full of all manner of technical terms my definition of the sport was simply that

'Golf is a deliciously old fashioned game of integrity played professionally between the ears.'

However, twenty years ago golf was seen as being essentially a technical game full of a host of key terms relating to swings, rotations, and weight transferences, it was NOT THEN seen as a game that involved mental skills.

As well as an emphasis on mental skills, using Timeform as my model, I decided I would also give golfers symbols just as the Halifax firm famously gave horses symbols, for example they gave a squiggle to an un-genuine horse. Initially there were 15 golfer symbols, a figure that over the years rose to 20 in my final book in 2006, and they appeared next to the golfer's name in his player profile. They included an upturned bottle for a player who appeared to lack 'final round nerve', a birthday cake symbol to show a player who might show improvement because of a significant birthday, and a picture of a baby in a nappy to show the effects of The Nappy Factor when a player had become, or was soon to become a father.

So Elliott's Golf Form was born in 1994 with the final, and 13th edition, published in 2006.

The reaction to the book was very positive with Derek McGovern, then Sports editor of the Racing Post, writing forewords to all my first three books. In his foreword to the first book, he said that my 'ideas on the mental side of the game were refreshingly original ... what's more he backs up his claims with solid statistics', and in his foreword to the second he added that my ideas were not only 'refreshingly original they were also thought provoking and what's more they were backed up by numerous examples'. In the third he admitted that some of my ideas 'may have at first appeared a trifle ambitious but the proof was in the pudding. Elliott's meticulous research has uncovered a string of long priced winners'.

It is worth stressing that throughout the books I used the phrase mental skills rather than the term 'psychological' as I find a word that starts with 'psycho' is extremely off-putting to so many people as it conjures up thoughts of men in white coats together with images from Alfred Hitchcock's famous film. After all I believed that if professional sportsmen accepted help in training for developing relevant physical and technical sporting skills then it was surely logical for them to also accept help to develop their mental skills.

The University of Common Sense, 'mind over matter', and trick cyclists

For many years in the eighties and early to mid-nineties such an emphasis on and firm belief in the power and importance of mental skills was ridiculed by many of the 'old school' who felt threatened by something they didn't understand and didn't want to understand. The sign of intelligence is knowing what you do know and knowing what you don't know. However, many traditionalists 'didn't know that they didn't know' as they dismissed mental skills as nothing more than our old friend 'common sense' with the meaningless umbrella phrase 'it's mind over matter' regularly used. Indeed psychologists were ridiculed by referring to them as 'trick cyclists'.

Today there are still dinosaurs who can't cope with the emphasis on mental skills that has exploded in the 20 years since my first book was written. Indeed there are still those who don't know they don't know! Let's take just one example to illustrate the point. It comes from a retired football player, who has been a manager at top clubs and is still today an analyst on Sky TV.

'It's always best to expect the worst so you're never disappointed'

This is typical of those who have graduated from the University of Common Sense. Superficially it seems a statement that is OK. However, it is based on the view that it is always best to avoid disappointment which if you think it through means it is always best to have low expectations because if things go wrong you are therefore never disappointed, and if they go well you feel the joy of a pleasant surprise.

As you can see the focus of this 'common sense' statement is not on positive goals, not on fulfilling potential, not on maximising performance but on the negative, on avoiding disappointment and upset.

Those who accept and follow this 'common sense' phrase are simply unaware that

You move towards what you think about

After all what do you think accident-prone people think about?

So if you keep expecting to shoot wide as a football striker you probably will, or even worse, you will probably prefer to pass to a team mate even if he's in a poorer position to score.

So if you keep expecting to miss the putt rather than hole it you will almost certainly be proved correct

Jamie Spence who was a successful two time winner on the European Tour is now a top class Sky TV golf analyst, and he wrote a glowing foreword for Elliott's Golf Form 2005. At one point late in his career Jamie, who had never shot a single hole in one in his entire pro career, decided to discuss the matter with a hypnotherapist whose advice was to use visualisation techniques to see the ball going into the hole as he stood on the tee. In the third tournament after this advice he had his first hole in one, and, guess what, he had another the very next week!! By seeing the ball going in the hole he had actually reinforced his belief that it was possible.

That hole in one is just one example of how mental skills can and do improve sporting performance.

THE DOUBLE GENERATIONAL IMPACT OF MENTAL SKILLS
Mental skills have changed the younger sportsmen

This was most noticeable in golf which was a sport dripping in tradition in which age and experience was deeply respected. One side effect of that reverence was that younger players 'knew' that winning took time because it required several years to understand your own game, to develop course management skills, and gain the understanding necessary to adapt your game to the different courses. So younger players in that sense knew their place.

That was to change as players used the services of 'mind gurus' so their belief grew that they could win and do so when relatively young.

The growth of American College golf with coaches emphasising the crucial mental side of the game and teaching mental skills techniques was very significant in producing new 'breeds' of players prepared to win as young golfers.

And, of course, there was Tiger Woods who showed that age wasn't a barrier to success and that disciplined mental focus, symbolised by his final round blood red shirt, was possible even for young players.

Mental skills have rejuvenated the older players.

However, the older golfers also found that it was possible to improve their play by focusing on their minds as well as on their swing, and with modern equipment also giving them greater distance as they got older, we find that 'the golden oldies' were capable of much improved performance in their 40s.

Indeed we will see plenty of examples of this in Chapter 3 on the impact that landmark birthdays, such as the 40th, and indeed the 50th can have.

Mental skills are now popular because they work.

Now the traditionalists are in retreat, and having been dismissed for so long, mental skills are now used in commerce, industry and throughout professional sport.

I've seen first-hand in business the difference the adoption of mental skills can have and the reason is clear. The 'easy going' days of the past have gone forever so today it's 'What's the bottom line?' with mental skills in business being judged solely on whether they work, and because they do work their use has grown.

One particular field called Neuro Linguistic Programming or NLP has been extremely influential. I first studied it in the nineties and found it fresh, exciting, and very helpful. So whenever you hear of a sportsman whose form has been transformed by a Sports psychologist it is probable that NLP has been involved.

One interesting point to note is that in Asia the acceptance of an emphasis on mental fitness shows itself in different ways as sportsmen tend to use yoga and meditation as well as the more western Sports psychology and NLP.

Indeed today in virtually all individual and team sports the importance of mental skills to improve performance is internationally widely recognised.

Ernie Els — an early example of the impact of using a mental skills guru for the first time

South African star golfer Ernie Els had won in every year from 1994-2000 including two Majors, both US Opens. However, in 2001 he didn't post a single win on either the US or European tours.

What made matters worse for the 'Big Easy' was that his fellow South

African Retief Goosen, by contrast, had played superbly well in 2001 winning the US Open as well as two European tour wins with Retief's use of sports psychologist Jos Vanstiphout making a huge difference to the Goose's form. A good example of Jos' influence came in the 2001 US Open. On the final green in the final round Goosen three putted from nine feet to 'throwaway' a winning chance, and so he had to return to face a play off the following day. However, after a session with Jos, Retief relaxed and went out on Monday to win the play off comfortably beating Mark Brooks by two strokes.

Later in Chapter 7 we will look at Inspiration by Comparison, the process by which one sportsman compares himself to others to his own benefit, and there is no doubt that Els copied Retief when he also decided to work with Vanstiphout from September 2001 as 'I get a little agitated and a little irritated with myself and my game ... I wasn't calm inside ... I was fighting with myself.'

In that 2001 autumn, after starting using mental skills advice for the first time, Ernie showed his best form of the year when he finished 2nd in both the Tour Championship in America, and the Dunhill Links on the European tour. So I wrote, in my golf annual, that 'In 2002 this fresh emphasis on mental skills will, I believe, have a galvanising effect on Ernie so 'I expect Ernie to win at least twice and play really well in the season's first 3 majors, any one of which he could win'.

That prediction that Els' first use of mental skills would work proved to be 'spot-on' as Ernie took his game to a higher level in 2002 when he won his second major, the Open Championship as well as having four other wins — three on the European tour and one on the USPGA tour. It was the start of a successful relationship that would last for several years.

Jos Vanstiphout suffered a heart attack and died in December 2013 and Ernie's reaction to that sad news told its own story — 'He meant so much to my career. We really connected and there was a genuine love for each other there. He taught me to think in a certain way, and was so good for me. He really helped me win that 2002 Open, no question. We probably won 25 tournaments together in a short period. He didn't have the education, but he understood the psychology of how things worked and gave that to me.' Finally Ernie added that 'I will be forever grateful to him for that. He changed my life and I am really going to miss him. I know you shouldn't have regrets but I regret not seeing him before he left us'.

Now let's move on to TEN very recent examples of sportsmen and women from SIX different sports who have successfully used FIVE different mental skills gurus.

The sports are Football, Cycling, Skiing, Golf, Snooker and Rugby Union.

2001-2009: Football — Carlo Ancelotti

Carlo Ancelotti was the highly successful head coach of AC Milan from 2001-2009 winning the Champions League in 2003 and 2007, and Serie A in 2004.One of the changes he introduced was 'the Mind Room' which was overseen by his assistant, Bruno Demichelis who was a sports psychologist. It was designed to relax players encouraging them to stay calm as they watched their performances, both good and bad, It allowed players to improve their resilience through mental training, and given Milan's success under Ancelotti it clearly worked well.

2010: Skiing — Lindsey Vonn

The blonde ski racer Lindsey Vonn was under enormous pressure as the American pin-up girl of the 2010 Vancouver Winter Olympics especially as she had suffered a serious shin injury in the build up to those Games. However, she had worked closely with the senior US psychologist Sean McCann who had Lindsey regularly visualising how she would perform and how she would appear when receiving the Gold medal on the rostrum. 'You move towards what you think about' so no surprise that in her first event she won the Gold medal in the downhill, and so became the first ever American to triumph in that race.

Today Lindsey is well known as Tiger Woods's girlfriend.

2010: Golf — Louis Oosthuizen

Louis had been in very poor form in the build up to the 2010 Open shown by his form figs of 77-MC-21-20-MC-WD-68. However, after working with Karl Morris, a Manchester Sports psychologist he was given a new, if simple, technique to help him focus. Louis' pre shot routine had been poor so Karl suggested that he should have a visible 'red spot' and to focus on it before swinging or putting and this enabled the South African by focusing on the 'red spot' to eliminate negative thoughts.

The technique worked superbly as Louis, who started as a 250/1 rank outsider, pulled away from the field at St Andrews to win his first major convincingly by seven clear shots in a classic example of the effectiveness of mental skills.

2014: Rugby Union — Danny Cipriani

Danny, as we'll see in detail later in Chapter 9 on The Comeback Trail, had had a troubled career after he was dropped from the England side in 2008. However, six years later in 2014 he decided to change his lifestyle, and focus on his Rugby in a determined effort to play for England again. His first step was to seek help from mental skills guru Steve Black who as Chris Foy, Rugby Correspondent of the Daily Mail, pointed out set Danny various tasks including keeping a daily journal, and reading various books relating to mental skills, with the key intention of getting Danny to think about decision making, after all as a fly half he has to make quick decisions as a key part of his rugby role. Danny's career turnaround got its reward when he went on England's

New Zealand tour in early summer 2014. However, he was controversially omitted from the national squad for the Autumn test campaign.

2014: Golf — Steve Bowditch

Steve Bowditch was a 30-year-old Aussie who had only twice been in contention to win in the 110 tournaments he'd played on the USPGA tour before in March 2014 he won the Texas Open as a 300/1 outsider. After his victory he'd said that he'd seen a sports psychologist for the first time the day before the tournament began. At first he wouldn't reveal the name of the person who turned out to be Angela Pampling, wife of tour player Rod, who had worked with tour players before including Michael Sim.

As we'll see in Chapter 7 on Inspiration by Comparison it could be he was also inspired by other first time winners including Aussies like himself, yet it was surely not just a coincidence that he posted his first win immediately after his first use of mental skills.

In recent years sports psychiatrist Dr. Steve Peters has rapidly become the go-to mental skills guru for all top British sportsmen with his superb book, The Chimp Paradox, becoming a best seller.

So our final five examples involve work he has done in three different sports.

2008: Cycling — Victoria Pendleton

Victoria had under-performed big style in the 2004 Athens Olympics when she had been overwhelmed by the whole experience. So she spent a lot of time with Dr. Steve Peters who was the sports psychiatrist working for the British cycling team. 'I was a mess. I really was down, it took me about a year with Dr. Peters to get my head working in the right direction'. Going from rock bottom in Athens to the Gold medal she won in Beijing in 2008 was testimony to her mental skills work as shown in her own admission that 'I don't think I would have realised my potential without Steve.'

2011: Football — Steven Gerrard

Liverpool captain Stevie G. in 2011 was suffering from a serious groin avulsion injury, and feeling really low he took the advice of one of Liverpool's physios who told him that he should see a mental skills expert, and that Dr. Steve Peters was the best. So doctor Steve met captain Steve, and the captain has been very impressed. 'I can only speak very highly of my private one-on-ones with him...I am a lot more patient as a person now... he's also helped my game...he helps with positivity, the power of thought and staying upbeat.'

Playing in a new deeper position Stevie G. had a very good 2013/14 season scoring 13 Premier League goals, and making 13 assists with Liverpool finishing second in the Premier League so ensuring the return of Champions League football to Anfield.

2012: Football — Craig Bellamy

Craig had played for Liverpool in the 2006 and 2007 seasons before he returned to play for the Reds under manager Kenny Dalglish in August 2011. However, just three months later he was deeply affected by the suicide of his great friend Gary Speed, and he was also going through a marriage break down so the striker with a reputation as a real 'firebrand' turned to Dr. Peters. 'Bellers' later said that 'The Steve Peters thing is responsible for my form at the moment' after he scored in seven consecutive games. He became a calmer, more disciplined player and in his autobiography he said that 'Not one single person in the world has ever made more sense to me than him.'

2012: Cycling — Sir Chris Hoy

Chris joined up with Dr. Steve Peters in 2003 and a year later in Athens Chris won the first of his six gold medals. The Scotsman went on to win three more golds in the 2008 Beijing Olympics, and another two in London in 2012, and Chris was very clear that Peters' mind programme 'helped me win my Olympic Golds'.

2012/14: Snooker — Ronnie O'Sullivan

Ronnie is widely recognised as the best ever snooker player but he has always been a deeply conflicted character. Referring to snooker he's said that 'Sometimes I detest it so much I can't look at a cue yet the sport has always been the love of my life.' Ronnie had won three World Championships when he considered retirement in 2011 however, with the help of Dr. Peters he renewed his love affair with snooker and went on to win back to back World Championships in 2012 and 2013. He said afterwards he owed a huge amount to his meetings with Dr. Steve Peters, which had 'made a massive difference in my life.'

As an example of their relationship when defending his World Championship in 2014 Ronnie was losing overnight in a second round match 9-7 to Joe Perry so he contacted Dr. Peters and next morning the good doctor travelled to Sheffield. 'I really appreciated it...he said a couple of things I should take on board and I did and it made a massive difference'. Ronnie then went on to win that match 13-11 after winning the final four frames!

However, in the final Ronnie was beaten by an inspired Mark Selby, and we'll return to Mark's superb achievement and the basis of his inspiration in Chapter 4 on The Funeral Factor.

Let's now look at examples of teams using mental skills gurus.

2013/14: Football — Liverpool

After working successfully for the then performance director of British Cycling David Brailsford, helping as we have seen Sir Chris Hoy, Victoria

Pendleton and others like Sir Bradley Wiggins to considerable success, Dr. Peters was asked by Liverpool manager Brendan Rogers to join his team at Anfield. So he started working at the club usually for one day a week, and he also watched matches partly to analyse players' 'impulse management', and to see how they react in 'pressure situations'.

Steve Peters works with Brendan Rogers finding out what the manager wants him to achieve, and follows that up with one-to-ones and collective meetings with the players. The guru has a reputation for personal warmth, simple language, and being a really good listener, and he uses his 'Inner Chimp' model to enable players to understand what is going on mentally when, for example they lose confidence, feel angry, or impatient. However, he knows his own boundaries so he never gets involved in tactics or the technical side of the game.

The proof of the pudding lies in the positive reaction of the players and the team results as there can be absolutely no doubt at all that Dr Peters has had a major impact. For example Raheem Sterling has said that 'the way he works is brilliant ... on the outside you may think it's complicated but all the messages are very straightforward,' and the pacy striker realised that, 'I'd stopped being natural, stopped doing all the things that I'd done which got me into the first team in the first place.' As a result his performance levels improved considerably and he forced his way not only back into the Liverpool team but also into the England team that started the 2014 World Cup.

It is surely no coincidence that helped by working with Peters both Jordan Henderson and Daniel Sturridge had their best ever seasons, and they too played in the World Cup. Let's also remember that 'bad boy' Luis Suarez, after returning from his ban in September 2013, not only played extremely well but was also so well behaved on the field that both the football writers and his fellow pros made him their Player of the Year, and we have already seen how deeply captain Steven Gerrard has been impressed by the 60-year-old guru. So it seems fair and accurate to say that Liverpool's best ever Premier League season was in part due to the influence of a mental skills guru and his 'Inner Chimp'.

2014: World Cup — England for the first time take a sports psychiatrist with them

Although he had never before used a mental skills guru in his career England manager Roy Hodgson decided to take Dr. Steve Peters to Brazil. Hodgson knew all about Peters' impact at Anfield and his work with England captain Steve Gerrard so he felt that what Peters had done for Liverpool he could also do to some extent over a shorter period with the national team. Another key reason was that as England had a really abysmal record in penalty shoot-outs in the big International tournaments the presence of a guru like Dr. Peters would provide vital relevant mental skills help in handling those pressure situations.

While in Brazil the players were not forced
although many did because they knew that car
five Liverpool players in the squad rated him
Rooney who had also met Peters a few times before
seemed to sum up the general view that, 'He's a great ben.
England's results however, were disappointing as they finis.
of their group and so were eliminated before the knock out stage.
matches could be decided on penalties. It was surely a sad coincidence u.
the first time the FA had taken a mental skills guru to a major tournament
the team's results were poor.

2014 — Dr Steve Peters continues as Euro 2016 qualifying starts with a convincing win in Switzerland

England wisely continued to use Dr. Steve Peters' services for the Euro 2016 qualifying matches that started in September 2014. England's coach Gary Neville, writing in his Daily Telegraph column, said that, 'over the years I have seen young players overwhelmed by fear of the consequences when things go wrong. It really bites you. The mental side of playing for England is different and we can no longer leave anything to chance.' So every England player had a 30 minute private one-to-one with the good doctor, and it sure seemed to help as England convincingly won a potentially tricky away match 2-0.

The relevance of Mental Skills to Sports analysis

There are FOUR key reasons why the simple act of visiting a sports psychologist can produce significantly improved performance.

1. It shows a real determination and commitment to improve performance, which in itself can act as a motivating factor because if you have chosen to try something new you have extra motivation as you really want to make it work.

2. It will provide insights, understandings, and increased self-awareness which can create greater control, calmness and composure especially in pressure situations.

3. Specific techniques, skills and practices can be followed causing the reduction or elimination of negative thoughts.

4. A model, such as Dr. Peters' Inner Chimp, can be used that is applicable to other non-sporting life situations so that benefits can occur both on and off the sporting field.

So when analysing any sporting event it's wise to make a note of those individuals or teams that are using mental skills assistance especially if it's for the first time.

When assessing the possible result of any sporting event, whether in an individual or team sport, apart from the obvious although important, factors past and recent results, injury news, and the weather we need to find t which individual or team is likely to be highly motivated, which most kely to produce an average performance and which will underperform.

So let's start on our journey through the more unusual aspects of sporting motivation by looking in the next three chapters at how births, birthdays, and deaths can act as motivating factors.

CHAPTER TWO
THE NAPPY FACTOR

THE BIRTH OF THE NAPPY FACTOR

"It's a boy ... you're a father...I cried as the 7lb 8oz bundle entered the world. I was all at once overcome by excitement, pride and a sense of responsibility.

I felt as if I was the first father ever with the only baby ever born".

They were the words I used to introduce The Nappy Factor in my second Golf Form book back in 1995.

The idea had been floating around in my head ever since the birth of my two sons, Steven [1978] and Martin [1980]. I was present at their births and the experience, excitement and exhilaration I felt was extraordinarily strong.

However, while exhilaration remained, I felt a much greater sense of responsibility and so took a hard look at my working life before taking important decisions to develop and expand my skills and activities.

I then began to realise that if the whole effect of becoming a father could energise me into significant personal development then it could surely also energise sportsmen. So I began to see if there were any sporting examples, and as 'You see what you look for' I was genuinely pleased, but not surprised, to find not just some but countless examples covering several sports.

SONS AND DAUGHTERS

One question arises: does it make any difference whether the baby is a son or a daughter?

I would expect that in the majority of cases a father wants a son, and a mother wants a daughter although a lot will depend on the family's existing gender balance. If a couple already have, say, two or three sons then they would be more likely to want a daughter if they have another child. This was well illustrated by David and Victoria Beckham who after having three sons six years later had a daughter Harper Seven.

Initially The Nappy Factor referred to the positive impact on a sportsman that the birth of a first child would have especially if it was a boy as it seems likely that most sportsmen would prefer their first child to be a son.

So let's start our journey through the impact that births have had on sportsmen by looking at.

THE EARLY HISTORY OF THE NAPPY FACTOR AND THE REACTION TO IT
In golf

Among the many examples I gave when discussing the 'Nappy Factor' all those years ago in my golf books were the following 'Magnificent Seven'.

- The Australian golfer Tim Elliott [no relation] had struggled for over ten years. Nearly broke and without a win he became the father of twins in early 1994, and within five weeks of their birth he was in sensational form winning the Players Championship and the South Australian Open with a record score, and he won more money in those five weeks than he had done in the previous ten years!!

- In 1995 there had been six winners on the European Tour who had won a tournament within 12 months of becoming a father, and they certainly weren't short priced favourites as they won at odds of 40/1[twice] 66/1,80/1,100/1 and 125/1!

There were also five big name major winning golfers on the USPGA Tour

- **Arnold Palmer.** First child, a daughter in 1956 — in 1957 his career really takes off with 4 wins.

- **Greg Norman.** His second child and only son born 1985 — wins his first major in 1986 when he topped the US money list.

- **Jack Nicklaus.** First child, a son born 1961 — wins 1962 US Open, the first of his 18 Major wins!

- **Larry Mize.** Son born in 1986 — the following year he wins the US Masters.

- **Steve Elkington.** First child a daughter born in March 1995, and within 6 months 'The Elk' had won his first and only major, The USPGA, and later in February 1997 Steve became a father again this time of a son, and in his first three tournaments after the birth of his son, Steve won twice — winning the Doral Ryder Open at 50/1, and then he led from start to finish to win the prestigious Players' Championship at 40/1.

Although golf was the focus of my books there were Nappy Factor examples given from other sports.

In football
Manchester United and England star Paul Ince showed much improved form after the birth of his son Thomas in January 1992. Tom is now also a successful professional footballer.

In snooker
Steve Davis became 'Daddy Davis' in early 1993 and went on a run of 10 unbeaten world ranking matches and won the British Open.

In horseracing
Jockeys' agent Peter Harris in 1996 when asked who was the person he owed most to in his life replied, 'My daughter, although she does not know it yet. Since I knew she was on the way, I've got my act together more.'

In lawn tennis

In 1995, when he reached the Wimbledon men's singles final, Boris Becker publicly stated that his renaissance was inspired by the arrival of his son Noah who was born in January 1994.

The Nappy Factor continued to work in the early years of the new millennium.

- **Andrew Oldcorn** became a first time father of a daughter, Natasha, in 2000 and I was very grateful to journalist Nick Dye for sharing with me an interview he did with Andrew, after the third round of the 2001 Volvo PGA when the 41-year-old held a five shot lead. In it Nick specifically referred to The Nappy Factor as Andrew had told him that he felt different now that he's a dad ... less erratic, more relaxed and glad of a golf break from domestic work. Oldcorn led from halfway, kept his nerve, and after his shock 150/1 win said he was 'totally in control'. It was a victory that proved that The Nappy Factor can significantly improve performance even when the first child is a daughter.

- **Darren Clarke** became a first time father of a son in 1998 and of a second son in 2000 and he stated categorically 'that my perspective on life now has completely changed'. Notice that Darren said 'completely' ... and it sure impacted on his golf as he showed when winning his first World Golf Championship, the WGC Accenture Matchplay, as an 80/1 outsider in February 2000 and he'd had to beat both of the world's two top-ranked players, Tiger Woods and David Duval, to do so.

- **Michael Campbell** attributed his run of 5 wins in 12 months culminating in his 28/1 win in the 2000 German Masters to the effect of becoming a first time father of a son. The New Zealander, after his breakthrough 66/1 win in the 1999 Johnnie Walker Classic, said that 'My son Thomas inspired me to this victory.'

- **John Daly** has had such a controversial and colourful career that it has been forgotten that he was a classic example of The Nappy Factor when he totally changed his attitude after becoming a first time father of a son in 2003. JD became a 'new' man, he lost 3 stones in weight, and said goodbye to his gripit'n'rip style of play. In 2004 he stated that 'I could probably hit it 30 yards further, but I wouldn't be able to control it.' So the player who was once the longest driver on Tour had taken stock of his situation, and put his macho image in the fridge as he set about regaining his form as he hadn't won for 9 years! Guess what? In Feb 2004 on his very first start he was the 150/1 shock winner of the Buick Invitational, after a 3 man play-off, beating a very strong field including Tiger Woods, Vijay Singh and Phil Mickelson.

- **Ernie Els**' successful use of mental skills guru Jos Van Stiphout was alluded to in the last chapter. However, the Nappy Factor was also very important in his rise to the very top in world golf when he became the father of a son for the first time in Oct 2002 [he already had a daughter] so his Nappy Factor year was 2003 and Ernie was 'on fire' from very early in the year as he won in his first two US tournaments and in two of his first four European events in a year in which he would post 8 wins worldwide. Sadly his young son Ben was later to change Ernie's life in another unexpected way when he was diagnosed as autistic.

REACTION TO THE NAPPY FACTOR

Reviewers, critics and golf writers were attracted to The Nappy Factor by its catchy name together with its originality. Remember we are talking about almost 20 years ago so I knew that there were those from the 'old school' who heard the phrase, laughed and almost dismissed it out of hand. Nevertheless it was subject to analysis and comment in the leading papers and journals of the time.

The golf writers in the leading golf journals and in the national press referred to the concept in their reviews

There was one writer who seemed determined to misunderstand the point and rubbish the idea. It was Peter Watts writing in the Sunday Times on 6th April 1996 who wrote 'Steve Elkington put his success in last week's Players Championship down to the Nappy Factor which states that new fathers are likely to win their next tournament because of the added responsibility they feel. Against this is the Bloody Kids Syndrome which lasts on-and-off for the next 18 years and has a less favourable effect.' Apart from getting The Nappy Factor completely wrong, as it doesn't say that a player will win his next tournament, Watts's negative words probably told us much more about the writer than they did about the subject, about which he'd clearly done absolutely no research.

By contrast the reaction from the professional golf writers in the leading golf journals was very different and very favourable. Indeed Colin Callender in Golf Monthly wrote that 'there is ample evidence to suggest that the arrival of a new child can actually improve your game.'

However, let's leave the last word to that doyen of golf writers Peter Dobereiner who wrote an article in Golf World in March 1996 under the heading 'The Nappy Factor gets the nod', and as always with Peter it was thoroughly detailed, and he'd clearly researched the subject deeply himself. With permission the article was reproduced in full in Elliott's Golf Form 1997 on pages 49 and 50. His conclusion was that, 'None of the individual examples prove anything by themselves. But the accumulating body of evidence — and there is plenty more where that came from — does seem to establish a link between fatherhood and achievement.'

ACADEMIC BACKING FOR THE NAPPY FACTOR

The articles by Colin Callender in Golf Monthly and especially the one by Peter Dobereiner in Golf World were very encouraging. However, another big boost came from a most unexpected source.

In June 2000 in Milan there was a world conference of Labour Economists and their main research findings were featured in *The Independent* by Cherry Norton, the paper's Social Affairs editor, on the 19th June.

A study using research based on data from 1968-1993 covering over 1,200 men had reached three main findings

1. **Men's salaries rise by nearly 5% every time they have a child, with the 'fatherhood premium' being far greater for a son than for a daughter.**

2. **Economists found that men whose first child is a son earn 8% more than men who father a daughter.**

3. **Each second and subsequent son raises the father's earnings by 3% more than each second and subsequent daughter.**

GOLF ANALYST BACKS THE NAPPY FACTOR

If the support from the academic world was surprising then the next pillar of support came completely 'out of the blue' when on 12th June 2006 I received an email from top golf analyst and tipster Dave Tindall who had been writing Golf Previews on the Internet since 1997.

Dave, who you will have come across already in his Foreword for this book, was a psychology graduate and so had always been interested in the mental side of the game and hence in ideas such as The Nappy Factor.

2006 was to be a mega year for Dave because on April 2nd his wife gave birth to their first child, a boy Joe, 'I joked at the time that I wondered if The Nappy Factor worked for golf tipsters as well as for players', and Dave went on to tell me that after a mixed season 'things have gone crazy' and 'whether it is coincidence or not, it was the most concentrated spell of profits I've ever had since I started betting on golf in 1994.'

I can vouch for Dave's selections that followed his return to work in late April when in a six-week, nappy-inspired period Dave had the following great run of results:

- 7th May — Wachovia Championship: Jim Furyk W 20/1
- 14th May — Byron Nelson: Brett Wettterich W 125/1
  and Adam Scott T3rd 20/1
- 21st May — Irish Open: Thomas Bjorn W 33/1
- 9th June — Barclays: Vijay Singh W 20/1

Dave has two children and while his wife was pregnant with their second child, daughter Alice, who was born in May 2009, he had his second most successful spell of golf punting with Ryan Palmer and Angel Cabrera being his big 150/1 winners. As Dave said recently to me, 'Does The Nappy Factor extend back to pregnancy. Some similar themes I guess.' This point is an important one to which we'll return later in this chapter.

So here we have a psychology honours graduate who understood the Nappy Factor and found that after the birth of his first child, a son, The Nappy Factor was at work, and that it returned when his wife was pregnant with their second child, a daughter.

The Nappy Factor, 'the new secret of golf betting', can be a potent weapon in the battle to beat the Bookies

The Nappy Factor may be interesting yet one question is how important is it in analysing sport and can it give punters an edge in the battle against the bookies? Peter Dobereiner in Golf World had called The Nappy Factor 'the new secret of golf betting', and he was right as it can be a very potent, predictive weapon in the battle to beat the bookies. There have been several examples over the years of the betting opportunities that have been opened up by the Nappy Factor. However, there was one outstanding example that is 'on the record' as I predicted it in one of my golf books — it was in a high profile Major a decade ago.

It was at Augusta in 2004 when Phil Mickelson won his very first major in his Nappy Factor year after the birth of his first son Evan Samuel in March 2003.

The conventional wisdom at the end of 2003 was that Mickelson 'had gone at the game', that he was obsessed by length off the tee. After all he hadn't even made the top 30 on the US Money list for the first time ever, and so didn't qualify for the season ending 2003 Tour Championship. He ended that year ranked 189th for driving accuracy, 107th for greens in regulation with no wins, and apparently no hope!

Not surprisingly he was written off by the bookies with 33/1 on offer in October 2003 for the following year's US Masters when I gave him to members of my sports service as a strong ante post bet for two key Nappy Factor reasons.

First, he did have some 'previous'. His only previous winless year as a pro was in 1999, and in that year Phil had focused on his new fatherhood rather than his golf with his first child, daughter Amanda arriving in the June of that year. However, the following year in 2000 in a new Millennium and in his first full Nappy Factor year his form had taken off 'big style' as he won 4 times finishing 2nd on the US Money list.

Second, I expected that Phil would reflect on the way he'd wasted his huge talents in 2003, and surely he wouldn't want his new son coming to him in future years asking 'Why have you never won a major, daddy?' Lefty had the 'bottle', and with his game so well suited to Augusta he would surely quietly reflect and show a completely new approach in 2004. My expectation was proved correct as he was 'on fire' in his first eleven events in which he won twice and posted five other top five finishes.

However, the 'biggee' came at Augusta in the US Masters when my player profile conviction that he'd fight out the finish with Ernie Els came true. I'd written in Elliott's Golf Form 2004 that 'I can see him fighting out the finish with Ernie Els', and that 'I can visualise an emotional Mickelson holding his young son after winning his first Major, the US Masters.' He did win with Ernie second one shot back. However, I'd got it wrong as, after his win, it was his daughter Amanda he held up not his son!!

On that never to be forgotten evening Phil's win showed not only that the Nappy Factor was valid but that it could also be successfully used as a powerful predictive weapon against the bookies. No prizes for guessing which player was on the front of the following year's golf annual!

That was a decade ago and there have been others since in lesser lower profile events but Phil the Thrill's 33/1 success was the most satisfying because it was predicted well in advance and at a time when most pundits had written him off.

The Nappy Factor has continued to work in recent years

Here are EIGHT examples covering FOUR sports — Golf, Football [Premier League and La Liga], Rugby Union, and Lawn Tennis.

- **2009: Wayne Rooney** became a first-time father of a son, Kai Wayne, whose arrival in November had a massive impact on his father's form. The Manchester United star went on in that 2009/10 season to score 4 goals in a Premier League game for the first time, score his first hat trick for 3 years, go on to score 26 Premier League goals, and overall he scored 33 goals in 43 European, Cup and Premier League games. Indeed his manger Sir Alex Ferguson called him 'a terror of a player' so no surprise then that he was the PFA's Player of the Year. In all the media words re Rooney's form there has been minimal mention of the Nappy Factor impact that inspired Rooney to his best ever season. Indeed his later poor performance in the World Cup in South Africa in the summer of 2010 was surely to a very significant degree caused by his isolation from his new son whose arrival had inspired such an excellent domestic season.

- **2010: Luke Donald** became a first time dad with a daughter Elle, and the following year his wife was pregnant with their second child, another daughter, who arrived in November. So 2011 was definitely Luke's Nappy Factor year, and what a truly amazing season it was as he reached world No 1, he won his first World Golf Championship, the Accenture World Match play, before going on to win the prestigious

BMW/PGA Championship at Wentworth and the Scottish Open on the European Tour. He needed to win the final US tournament, The Children's Miracle Network Hospitals Classic, to top the US Money list, and despite the pressure he was under he did just that, and so he ended that unforgettable year as the first player ever to win both the European and USPGA Money lists. The year however, had a bittersweet ending as Luke's father died in November in the same week that his second daughter was born.

- **2012: Jamie Donaldson** in the eleven years since joining the European Tour had played in 244 golf tournaments with no wins and just two 2nds, and two 3rds to show for all his efforts. That was all to change after March 2012 when his first child, a son Max was born. Just over three months later Jamie was the hugely impressive winner of the 2012 Irish Open after a superb final round 66, and then early in 2013 he won again in the Abu Dhabi Championship. The Welshman's two wins, and other fine performances in the first year since the birth of his son had rocketed Jamie up the world rankings to No 25 by mid-January 2014, and in interviews he later admitted that becoming a first-time father had been an important factor.

  Indeed in an article under the banner headline 'Having the kids turned me into a winner at last', Martha Kelner in a pre- Ryder Cup article wrote "If anyone can be presented as proof of the existence of the 'nappy factor' — a term introduced by betting guru Keith Elliott to suggest having babies, particularly boys, makes a better golfer — it is Donaldson".... How fitting that Jamie 12 days later went on to hole the winning putt for the European team!!

- **2012: Peter Hanson** already had a young daughter Stella when his second child, son Tim, was born in 2011, and in his first Nappy Factor season after his arrival the Swedish golfer took his game to new heights with his best ever year in 2012 in which he won twice on the European tour, he posted his best ever finishes in two of the US Majors when 3rd in the US Masters, and 7th in the UPGA, and in September he was a member of the successful European Ryder Cup team.

- **2013: Luis Suarez**, like Peter Hanson, already had a young daughter when his second child, a son Benjamin, was born in September 2013 in the week leading up to the away game against Sunderland. So it wasn't surprising that he scored twice in that match which Liverpool won 3-1. From then on he was 'on fire' in a season which ended with him easily the top goals scorer in the Premier League and winning both the PFA and the Sportswriters Player of the Year awards. Similarly to Wayne Rooney commentators tend to ignore the massive positive impact that the birth of his son had on Luis.

- **2014: Danny Care** is an England international rugby union player who has had what can best be described as a 'colourful past' associated with off field indiscretions. However, in 2014 the Harlequins scrum half played exceptionally well notably on February 22nd at Twickenham when his late match winning try enabled England to beat Ireland 13-10, after being 3-10 down. It was only after the match that Danny revealed that just two days before that game he had learned that his partner Jodie was pregnant and that they were expecting their first baby, and as he admitted 'it was definitely on my mind when I scored against Ireland'. He went on to speak of the deep significance of becoming a father, and the responsibilities it will bring saying he'd done the 'lad years' and that he was now excited to have a family when relatively young [he's 27] 'so my kids could watch me play rugby', and crucially he said that, 'Now there's a little Care Bear on the way, it's a special reason to play well.'

  His son Blake was born in October, and a week later 'Daddy Danny' celebrated by rocking his arms cradle style after he scored a vital try as Harlequins started their European Champions Cup campaign with a 16 point home win over Castres.

- **2014: Novak Djokovic** had lost 5 of his previous 6 Grand Slam finals yet in 2014 when he played in the Wimbledon singles final he beat Roger Federer to win for the first time in SW 19, and his win was surely due in large part to this being the 27-year-old's first Nappy Factor final as his fiancée Jelena Ristic was pregnant with their first child due in late October. Novak was clearly delighted as he said 'it's a new chapter in our lives and it gives me a lot of new motivation ... seeing her stomach grow day by day is a miracle really'. Shortly after his Wimbledon Triumph Novak and Jelena were married and their son Stefan was born in October.

- **2014: Angel Di Maria** was the big new signing by Manchester United in the summer of 2014 when he was bought for a British record fee of £59.7 million from Real Madrid after he had been in the form of his life in the previous season. He played really well all season and notably in the key end of season matches he scored when Real Madrid beat Barcelona in the final of the Copa Del Rey, and he was voted Man of the Match by UEFA in Lisbon when Real Madrid won the Champions League for the 10th time.

  However, the Nappy Factor was behind the Argentinian's best ever season as in April 2013 his daughter Mia was born three months prematurely and given just a 30 per cent chance of survival. But Mia survived and thrived and Di Maria himself acknowledged how important she had been to him when he said that **'she transmitted so much energy to me and it helped me to have the spectacular year that I have had.'**

Sunday September 14th: The Nappy Factor strikes twice with a transatlantic double

In Holland on the afternoon of September 14th Paul Casey won the KLM Open. Earlier on September 1st Paul had been presented with a baby boy, his first child, by his fiancé Polyanna Woodward so 'this was my first tournament as a dad, and my first win as a dad.'

Then just 7 hours later on the East Lake course in Georgia Billy Horschel won the season ending Tour Championship and the $10million bonus that went with it. After his win Billy said that, 'I had this sense of calm over me,' before he received a message from his heavily pregnant wife Brittany who tweeted a picture of herself smiling with hands on her belly .A few weeks later when present at the birth of his first child, daughter Skylar Lillian, Billy said her birth was "the biggest win of my life".

Saturday November 8th: The 'Double' Nappy Factor inspires FA Cup giant killing

Craig Mahon became a first time father of twin boys, Finlay and Sidney on the Friday evening before the 25-year-old winger was to play the following day in the first round of the FA Cup for non-league Chester FC at high flying division two club Southend. His wife insisted that he should play 'you'll have the rest of your life with your babies but you won't get many chances to play in the FA Cup so go and enjoy it.' So Craig made the 220 mile trip on Saturday morning and yes, you've guessed it ... he scored the winning goal with a superb left foot shot to give his team a giant-killing 2-1 win.

Craig's reaction was understandable. 'I've had twins, I've become a Dad, I've scored in the FA Cup and we've gone through and I can't put into words how I feel at the moment'. **It is the first example I've come across of The Nappy Factor inspiring a sportsman to instant success after a multiple birth.**

ASSESSING THE NAPPY FACTOR TWENTY YEARS ON

The Nappy Factor's popularity and longevity

The Nappy Factor is unquestionably the one concept that readers of my books and articles remember first. This was well illustrated in 2013 when I rang Mr. Paddy Power who runs the highly successful Irish bookmaking firm when he told me that he remembered my books and completely unsolicited he referred to the Nappy Factor.

So almost 20 years on let's make an assessment of this popular concept.

Sons and daughters

We have seen from Arnold Palmer in the 1950s through Andrew Oldcorn in 2001 and Luke Donald in 2010 that when the first child is a daughter the Nappy Factor can have a huge effect.

However, overall the evidence exemplified by Jack Nicklaus in the 1960s, Larry Mize in the 80s, John Daly in 2003, plus Wayne Rooney and Jamie

Donaldson in recent years suggests that the Nappy Factor is at its strongest when the first child is a son.

Together with the academic evidence we have seen it seems reasonable to suggest that the arrival of a son as a first child has a greater impact than that of a daughter

Two new amendments to the definition of The Nappy Factor are now needed

Originally the Nappy Factor referred to the positive impact becoming a father can have on a sportsman's performance. It was especially relevant to the initial impact that the FIRST child, especially if a SON, could have so its strongest impact would be in the first year AFTER the birth.

However, that original definition now needs two important amendments.

First the Nappy Factor can sometimes take effect BEFORE the birth once the pregnancy has been confirmed. We have seen examples this year with Wimbledon winner Novak Djokovic, Rugby Union star Danny Care, and golf's FedEx Cup winner Billy Horschel, and earlier with Dave Tindall and there are doubtless many other examples that remain outside the public domain. Compared to the time when I was so deeply affected by The Nappy Factor, today it is possible, if the prospective parents wish, to be told the sex of the unborn child. Today therefore this Pre Nappy Factor Pregnancy effect would be especially significant if it was known that the baby was to be the sex that the sportsman wanted.

Second, the birth of A SECOND CHILD AS A FIRST SON after the first child is a daughter can also have a dramatically strong Nappy Factor impact, with Greg Norman in 1985, Steve Elkington 1997, Ernie Els 2002, Peter Hanson 2012, and especially Luis Suarez in 2013/14, all classic examples. **Indeed it may well be that that this phenomenon has the greatest Nappy Factor impact of all** probably because it includes an element of sheer relief that 'at last I have a son'.

The Nappy Factor enters common parlance and is celebrated in the Premier League

It has been applied to sportsmen from different generations, different countries, and different sports, and it has clearly stood the test of time to such an extent that the Nappy Factor is now in common parlance.

I often see references to it in the Racing Post with the one on Saturday 30th November 2013 especially interesting as under the Nappy Factor heading it stated that 'Blyth Spartans Craig Hubbard has scored 10 goals in 12 games since the birth of his son Oscar'. Now I don't know how Craig celebrated those ten goals but it is surely worth noting that in recent years on the pitch in front of the TV cameras after a goal is scored a 'Bebeto' cradle-rocking celebration is nearly always used by millionaire Premier League players when the scorer has just become a father. Such a public celebration of fatherhood surely symbolises the importance of the Nappy Factor to today's sportsmen.

WHY DOES THE NAPPY FACTOR WORK SUCCESSFULLY SO OFTEN?

There is no doubt that becoming a father can have a strong positive effect on a sportsman for FOUR key reasons

- It provides a strong incentive to boost the family income.
- The sportsman wants his son or daughter to be proud of him.
- It provides a wider sense of perspective so a sportsman will be far less likely to mentally beat himself up after a poor result.
- It can enable a sportsman to mature and leave behind his 'jack the lad' days.

The fact that this also applies to non-sportsmen as well probably explains why the concept now appeals to so many people.

DOES THE NAPPY FACTOR APPLY TO ALL SPORTSMEN?

The 'Law of the Nappy Factor', unlike the Laws of Physics, is not one applicable in all circumstances. It is more like the Laws in Economics, which are statements of tendency, so there will be exceptions. For example the Nappy Factor certainly gave golfer Lee Westwood the 'swerve'. Lee's first child, Samuel, was born in 2001 and the top European golfer of 2000 then had his worst ever year in 2002.

There may be several reasons for this especially as initially after a birth there can be a 'disruption' effect that can counteract the Nappy Factor and this would especially be true if the arrival of the baby is followed by say a move to a new house, Also, of course other influences may be at work for example one or more of the new grandparents may become ill or the new parents themselves may start arguing about the details of their new life situation. So the Nappy Factor may not kick in straightaway and occasionally may not 'kick in' at all.

WHEN DOES THE NAPPY FACTOR START?

The impact can be immediate as we have seen with Wayne Rooney and Luis Suarez in football, Steve Elkington and John Daly in golf. It may take 3 months as with Jamie Donaldson while for others such as golfers Peter Hanson and Phil Mickelson it will be the next year.

FOR HOW LONG DOES THE NAPPY FACTOR LAST?

It may be a few months, even a year or more during which time a new higher level of performance is reached before it then plateaus, and possibly dips, but can then be sustained at a level higher than before the birth that triggered the Nappy Factor impact.

CAN IT BE USED WHEN BETTING?

Yes it can be very valuable although it is often best used when combined with other factors.

For example Phil Mickelson had the ideal game for Augusta and a winning temperament so the Nappy Factor became the key extra ingredient in the mix that made him such a great value bet.

Similarly with Luis Suarez we have a sportsman with not one but two special extra motivational forces working at the same time, the Nappy Factor and the Comeback Trail, which we'll discuss again in Chapter Nine, so it wasn't difficult to expect that, as a highly motivated and especially happy family man he would have such an excellent Premier League season.

As we continue our sporting motivational journey we now move from the Nappy Factor effect of the day of the birth, when a child first enters the world, to the motivating impact that later birthdays can have on sportsmen.

CHAPTER THREE
THE IMPORTANCE OF
LANDMARK BIRTHDAYS

The significance of landmark birthdays first hit me when, many moons ago, I worked part time as a tutor-counsellor for the Open University. The OU was set up to provide Degree level and other courses for adults who, although having the ability, had missed out in the past on higher education. What I noticed from the admittedly small sample of part time students who I worked with was the significantly high proportion who were aged 29 and 39, Why was that I wondered?

When discussing the students' reasons for joining the OU it was really noticeable that the 29- and 39-year-olds nearly all mentioned that they had reviewed their lives because they were about to hit the big 3-0 or the big 4-0.

Over the years our society has placed an increasingly greater emphasis on reaching 30, 40, 50, 60 and 70. With rising living standards, increasing disposable income, and longer life expectancy we have turned landmark birthdays into an ever expanding industry. Indeed if you are in any doubt just Google Landmark birthdays, and you will find a massive range of ways to spend your money. There is now a huge pressure on those approaching a Landmark birthday to create a memorable occasion as they hit the big three, big four, big five, big six, and even the big seven 0.However, the big thing about these big landmarks is not the big party but the big mental, emotional and motivational impact they can have on the birthday guy or gal.

AGEING TEN YEARS IN ONE DAY

As you cease to be 29, 39 or any of the other Nines mentally you seem to age 10 years in a single day. If you take becoming 40 as an example you not only cease to be in your thirties you actually enter your fifth decade and that change causes so many people to take stock of their careers, friends and marital status and as a result they often make very significant life changing and sometimes very regrettable decisions. A couple may decide to relocate to the country to remove themselves from the 'rat race', someone may look for a one night stand to see if they are still attractive, while others may decide to emigrate, or start a family. Sudden changes in careers, an extra marital affair, and moving house are often the result.

The key point about Landmark birthdays is that there is huge social, peer, and personal pressure to re-examine, re-evaluate and re-view your life in a way that simply does not happen with any other birthday. So let's be clear. The mental effects of becoming, say 29, 39 or 49 are real for so many people and the Landmark Birthday impact applies to sportsmen just as it applies to everyone else.

THE IMPACT OF THE NINES

I first wrote about the effects of landmark birthdays and the impact of reaching 39 and the other 'nines' in my first two golf annuals in 1994 and 1995. In the second of them I used the following three examples that had all occurred in the previous 12 months.

- The retirement of National Hunt jockey Steve Smith Eccles ...at 39.
- French politician Jacques Delors made a shock announcement that he wasn't to be a candidate in the French Presidential Election ... at 69.
- Former golf professional and TV commentator Clive Clark decided to stop facing the microphone in favour of joining Ernie Els in a design business ... at 49.

However, in my very first Golf annual I had also referred to

- The shock resignation of Liverpool manager Kenny Dalglish in February 1991 ... at 39 just ten days away from the big four-O.

In all the discussions regarding his shock resignation Kenny's age was never mentioned yet it may well have been a contributory factor.

1991: The Nines strike! — 39-year-old 'King' Kenny Dalglish resigns ten days before he's 40

As BBC Radio Merseyside's racing correspondent I used to broadcast live for 30 minutes every Friday night and although so many of those nights were memorable I'll never forget what happened on the third Friday in February 1991 because my racing slot and the whole of the evening's sports output was cancelled. The reason was the shock news had broken that Liverpool's manager Kenny Dalglish had resigned! On that night I can say without any doubt at all everyone, and I mean everyone, was in shock, nobody, not even Kenny's best friend Alan Hansen, had seen the resignation coming.

Two days earlier Liverpool had played at local rivals Everton in an epic FA Cup game in which Liverpool led four times yet only drew 4-4. Nevertheless on that Friday Liverpool were top of the league by three points and were still to replay against Everton in the FA Cup so Kenny's team were doing very well. So why did he resign?

'King Kenny' is revered on Merseyside as a footballer, as a manager but above all as a very special man because of his extraordinary involvement in the aftermath of the Hillsborough tragedy when he attended so many funerals. It was common knowledge that he had been very deeply affected by the media coverage, the disgraceful police handling of the situation that weekend, but above all by the shocking loss of the 96 lives.

So one theory was that he resigned because of the toll that Hillsboro had placed upon him, but that doesn't answer the question why resign then, why on that particular Friday night?

Years later he was to say that on the Wednesday in that Everton 4-4 game he could see that his defence needed to be shored up ...' I could see what needed to be done but I didn't act on it — that was the moment I knew I was shattered, I needed to get away from the pressure.' However, surely the effect of the pressure of his work as manager and the massive impact of his work for and with the Hillsborough families had been building up for some time. On a pressure scale of 0-100 it surely didn't go from zero to one hundred in one night at Goodison Park?

So perhaps there was another as yet unconsidered contributory factor as he resigned just ten days before his 40th birthday. Already drained by the pressures he'd been under perhaps the coming of that 40th birthday had already provided the opportunity to review his life as a result of which the thought of a break from those massive pressures he had been under by resigning at the end of the season had probably already occurred to him before being buried in his sub conscious.

Perhaps the loss of those four goals and his admitted subsequent indecision at Goodison Park had brought forward the idea of leaving from the end of the season.

So was it just a coincidence that Kenny was 39, just ten days away from his big four-0 birthday? Or was it, as I suspect, that the onset of that Landmark birthday played a significant part in his decision.

1998: The Nines strike again — 49-year-old Brian Kidd leaves to become a Premier League manager for the first, and only, time

Seven years after Dalglish's shock resignation there was to be another footballing example of the effect of the Nines!

Brian Kidd, on his 19th birthday, scored in Man United's famous 1968 European Cup winning side and was a good servant of that club till he left in 1974. After spells elsewhere he ended his playing career in 1984 and four years later he returned to Manchester United as youth team coach. Then in 1991 he was promoted by Alex Ferguson to become his assistant manager when the Premier League season started in 1992, and through the rest of the nineties decade United were extremely successful winning the FA Cup and Premier League double in 1994 and 1996,and the Premier League in 1993 and 1997.

However, when aged 49 years 7 months, in December 1998, he made the decision to leave United and go it alone when Blackburn Rovers, who had been Premier League winners three years earlier, asked him to manage their club.

Yes, there had been friction between Ferguson and Kidd following comments the United manager had made about Brian in his first book, but the timing of Kidd's move was probably heavily influenced by the thought that at 49 he was at a crossroads and so open to any new offer, any new challenge.

Sadly Brian couldn't save Rovers from relegation from the Premier League, and in November 1999 with Rovers 19th in Division One he was sacked after just 11 months in the job.

So here we have an example of a successful coach at a successful club taking a jump into the unknown and doing so at 49.

The ultimate irony was that six months after leaving United and three days before his 50th birthday Brian's former club won the European Cup and so became the first, and still the only, club ever to win the treble!!

2007: the Nines strike again — 29-year-old Jamie Carragher announces his retirement from international football — 'As I approached thirty I lost interest in being the dependable reserve.'

Star Liverpool defender Jamie Carragher who had won 34 international caps wrote in his autobiography that he decided to retire from international football for two key reasons. First, 'If I'd been England manager I'd have picked [John] Terry and [Rio] Ferdinand as first choice centre backs...the fact was I was too similar to Terry, He's a better version of me,' so Jamie knew if he continued with England he'd almost inevitably be a substitute.

Second, 'I'd rather add two more years to my Liverpool career than jeopardise this for England.'

So was Jamie's decision linked to the fact that he was 29, and the answer is a most definite 'Yes'. The approach of the 30th birthday is seen by many clubs as very significant as it is a common belief that outfield players are probably past their best as they have inevitably lost pace and so some clubs are often reluctant to offer players over 30 anything longer than a one year contract.

In Jamie's case he states with his usual honesty that being 29 was really significant, 'As I approached thirty I lost interest in being the dependable reserve' for England so he made the choice to focus solely on the club he loved rather than spending 'those long dreary afternoons in hotels...after heading off to Estonia, Russia, even London.' He no longer wanted to spend time travelling only to end up on the bench. Being 29 with his 30th birthday round the corner he knew that was the right time to make his decision, he made it, and he's never regretted it. With the Kop singing 'We all dream of a team of Carraghers' he played on for his beloved Liverpool till he retired at the end of the 2012/13 season after which he has successfully joined SKY TV as an analyst.

Having looked at the impact of the Nines let's now turn to the motivational effect of the key Landmark birthdays.

THE IMPACT OF THE 30TH, LIFE'S FIRST LANDMARK BIRTHDAY

Reaching the age of 18 marks the transition into adulthood. However, the first Landmark birthday as an adult comes 12 years later. The 30th birthday is the first birthday that we have as adults which enables us to review our overall situation, and to take stock of both our career and our personal life.

So having just examined the effects the Nines can have let's now look at the motivational impact that passing Landmark Birthdays can have so let's start with the first, the 30th birthday.

All sports are different however, there is one sport, golf, where although players may play well and win they can still improve as top golf players require so many different types of skill. On the technical side he needs to have developed skills in driving, iron play, chipping, pitching, bunker play, and putting, while adapting these skills to courses in different conditions from fast and firm to wet and slow. He must also develop the crucial mental skills to play well under pressure when at or near the top of the leaderboard. No wonder then that golfers, although often successful in their twenties, are often not at their best until they reach their thirties.

So it's to golf that we turn to see the very positive effects that the Landmark 30th birthday can have.

TWO GOLFERS WIN VERY IMPORTANT TOURNAMENTS THE DAY AFTER THEIR 30TH BIRTHDAY

Nick Faldo — 'One of my motivating things was that I turned 30 on the Saturday of the Open.'

Although a successful golfer who had five European Tour wins Nick Faldo spent the mid-1980s re-modelling his swing with his coach David Leadbetter. Nick had a swing that had, according to his coach, 'a number of faults' so Nick wanted to develop a swing that would withstand the pressures of major golf and he had a clear time scale in mind based on his landmark 30th birthday. Indeed he said 'I thought I had done my apprenticeship, I'd reached 30, I've got to start winning these majors.'

Nick's 30th birthday was on 18th July 1987 and that year it was the third day of The Open Championship at Muirfield. Nick said afterwards that he felt it was his time as he believed he would win his first major when he was in his thirties so when he won at Muirfield he was just thirty and he won on the first day of his fourth decade.

Nick went on to win two more Opens and three US Masters so ended his career with six major wins ... yet the key one, the one that opened the door to those other Major successes, was the one he won at Muirfield a day after that 30th candle was blown out the night before!

Scott [who?] Drummond at 500/1 wins the prestigious Volvo PGA as a Landmark birthday meets The Nappy Factor

Have you heard the story of the Scottish guy, with an English accent who in 2004 came into the mega rich Volvo PGA as fourth reserve and won at 500/1 the day after he was 30 and four weeks after he first became a dad?

Scott became a first time Dad in April 2004 when his daughter Kiera entered the world, and I knew he was such a proud first time dad as I'd received an EM telling me that he'd left a practice round at Wentworth playing with Matthew Blackey, a touring pro at Hayling, to be with little baby Kiera. However, during the Volvo PGA, like Faldo back in 1987, he was 30 on the Saturday of the tournament. On the final day Scott started one shot behind Angel Cabrera, and then, on his first day as a 30-year-old, playing relaxed quality golf he shot a superb eight under par 64 to win by two clear shots.

So we had the unique combination of the Nappy Factor and his first Landmark birthday coming together as two separate yet two interlocking forces that would motivate and relax Scott enabling him to win the biggest non-major on the European Tour calendar.

Throughout the tournament he had a calm, relaxed approach, top class course management and a 'hot' putter. So having won only £11,000 all year he received a cheque for over £440,000 and he shot up the world rankings from 435th to 95th — Scott was in the World's top 100 after the Nappy Factor had collided with a Landmark birthday!

Monty becomes the 'Emperor of Europe' once he reaches 30
Colin Montgomerie although he had finished 3rd in the European Tour's Order of Merit, the Tour's money list, in 1992 he hadn't won a single tournament that year, and indeed up to that point he'd actually won only twice in 138 starts on the Tour as a pro!

However, in 1993 Monty was 30 in June after which his form 'took off' with two wins in the second half of the year, and he won the Order of Merit [O/M] for the first time. It was to be the first of a staggering seven successive O/M titles that Monty was to win from 1993-1999 in a period in which he won 20 European Tour tournaments, and in that time he'd also posted three 2nd places in American majors.

There can be little doubt that Monty's form took off once he reached his thirties as he in effect became the Emperor of European golf for a Magnificent Seven successive years.

IN SPORT HITTING THE BIG FOUR-O CAN RELEASE AMBITION, DRIVE AND ENERGY
I know I am giving my age away but there was once a famous TV advert telling us that Phyllosan fortifies the over 40s. However, there is plenty of evidence to show that the effect of those 40 candles on the cake can do the job without help from any tonic!

However, in many sports the advancing years take their physical toll so we don't find examples of big improvements in performance because of the motivational impact of the big 4-0 in Football, Rugby Union, Rugby League, and American football. However, there is one sport where we do know that the landmark 40th birthday can have a definite impact on sporting performance, and that sport is golf.

IN GOLF THERE ARE NOW TWO FACTORS THAT ADD TO THE MOTIVATIONAL POWER OF THE 40TH BIRTHDAY

First the new technology with the modern clubs, irons, and balls have been especially helpful to the older pros as they can hit the ball further and so to some extent compensate for the advantage in driving distance that the younger pros would otherwise have.

Second, in America in the 'old' days when a player reached 50 he could join the Seniors Tour with other fifty plus guys who were known, for obvious reasons, as the 'round bellies'. However, the traditional game of golf was to be re-packaged and re-presented so the 'round bellies' Seniors Tour was consigned to history! After all the older players who were fifty and over were players who had almost certainly won in their earlier career so the Seniors Tour was rebranded in America as the new 'Champions Tour' with serious prize money. As a result there was a huge new incentive to keep your game as well your body and mind in top shape in your forties so that you could extend your career when reaching your fiftieth birthday.

Those two factors together with the liberating release of renewed drive, renewed ambition, and renewed energy have led to many golfers showing improved form and, in some cases, considerably improved form once that 40th candle has been blown out.

February 1997 — Mark O'Meara and Nick Price create a transatlantic piece of never to be repeated 40th birthday history!

On February 1997 we had the amazing example of two golfers, one on the European Tour, and the other on the USPGA Tour, who both won back-to-back tournaments in successive weeks in the month after they reached the big 4-0!

- On the European Tour Nick Price was 40 on the 28th January, and the following month he scored back-to-back wins winning the Dimension Data pro-am at 11/2 by eight shots on February 16th followed a week later with a win at 4/1, after a play-off, in the Alfred Dunhill South African PGA.

- On the American Tour Mark O'Meara hit the big 4-0 on the 13th January and he went on to win the AT+T Pebble Beach Pro-Am at 22/1 on February 2nd beating Tiger Woods by one shot, and then won the Buick Invitational at 12/1 the following week winning by two shots.

WILL THIS FEAT OF TWO GOLFERS ON THE TWO TOURS BOTH WINNING BACK TO BACK IN THE MONTH AFTER THEIR 40TH BIRTHDAY EVER BE REPEATED?

The answer is a resounding 'No' as today both tours have a much greater depth of talent than in the past. Especially in America there is an 'army' of excellent new young players most of whom have come through the American College system so they are usually long hitting, battle hardened, mentally strong players, and with the European Tour also stronger than in the past it would be truly astonishing if February 1997 was ever to be repeated.

The tale of the 40-year-old Ponytailed Peter Pan

However, probably the best examples of the effects of hitting the big four-O come from two European golfers.

Miguel Angel Jimenez is a wine drinking, cigar smoking, red Ferrari driving Spaniard who also plays excellent golf. He is a classic example of a larger than life sportsman who loves life, living it his way.

However, in his younger days he was seen as no more than a solid player so by the time he hit 40 in January 2004 although he was successful as he had seven wins in his 356 starts, a strike rate of 1.97%, he was not seen as an exceptional player. However, there was to be a startling transformation as once past the big 4-O in January 2004 Big-Mig, as he is affectionately known, won four times in that year alone, and he went on during his forties to win an amazing 13 times in 261 starts – a strike rate of 4.98% which is virtually a win every twenty starts! We'll return to Jimenez later in this chapter when we look at what happened when the Spaniard hit the big five-O.

The Great Dane who was 'Bjorn again' after hitting the big four-O

The other European player who showed considerably improved form once he blew out that 40th candle was the Danish golfer, Thomas Bjorn who was already a good player with nine wins when he was 40 in February 2011. Thomas celebrated early by winning the Qatar Masters twelve days before his birthday, and he went on to win three other tournaments in that year. Indeed in the three years after he hit the big 4-O 'The Great Dane' won five times before he was 43. No wonder the inevitable headline that he was 'Bjorn Again' was regularly seen.

THE POSITIVE IMPACT OF THE FINAL LANDMARK BIRTHDAY — THE 50TH

For obvious reasons the 50th is the last of the Landmark birthdays that can positively impact on sporting performance, and there is only one sport, Golf, in which passing that birthday can inspire players and we have three recent examples of this rare phenomena.

2007: Bernhard Langer

Langer had posted 40 European Tour wins and was a two time winner of the US Masters so he had a first class golfing CV when in August 2007 he hit the big 5-0 and decided to join the Champions Tour in America. Put simply he has taken that tour by storm dominating it totally as shown by his amazing stats as he won on his fourth start in 2007, and in his first full season in 2008 he won three times and he's gone on to be the Money List winner in six of the seven years up to and including 2014 during which time he has won 22 tournaments!!

On May 4th 2014 after his 20th win he said 'I feel like I am playing some of the best golf of my career.' He went on to play truly outstanding golf in the Seniors Open at Porthcawl when he won by an astonishing 13 strokes after an amazing final score of 18 under par. That superb performance was put into context by Tom Watson, who played in both The Open and the Seniors Open, when he said that Porthcawl played three shots per round tougher than Hoylake. Indeed Langer's brilliance led some commentators to ask if he should be a wildcard pick for the Ryder Cup in which he could possibly partner fellow German Martin Kaymer! Although the European Ryder Cup captain Paul McGinley did contact Bernhard the veteran German star was never going to gain a wildcard.

We will return to this extraordinary guy in Chapter 5 on The God Squad, and again in Chapter 8 on Mental Let Down.

2014: Miguel Angel Jimenez

We have already alluded to the charismatic Spaniard whose form dramatically improved after he was 40, and in 2014 on 5th January he was 50 but there was to be no pipe and slippers for Big-Mig!

He had ended 2013 by winning the Hong Kong Open so breaking his own record as the oldest player ever to win on the European Tour but he didn't return to action in 2014 until he played in the US Masters in mid-April in which he finished a superb tied fourth. Then a week later, having joined the US Champions Tour, he won his very first event, the Greater Gwinnet Championship by two shots. Then, after marrying a lady half his age, he went on to win his own national title, the Spanish Open in a three man play-off, and by that win on home soil he broke his own record to be the oldest ever winner, and the first player over 50 to win, on the European Tour.

In an amazing five-week spell he'd won on both sides of the Atlantic, played brilliantly to be placed at Augusta, and, of course, he'd been married!!!

This is surely the best-ever sporting example of the positive effects a Landmark birthday can have.

2014: Colin Montgomerie

Montgomerie was the golfer who we have seen set a record of winning the European Tour money list for seven successive years from 1993-1999 and although a multiple winner on the European Tour he'd never won in America, and he'd never won a major title although he'd been 2nd no fewer than five times! Butch Harmon once observed that the Scot 'could hear a fart on another fairway' as Monty often became distracted and was not too popular with American galleries. Indeed the jibe that he'd never won in the States and never won a major although true really hurt.

Throughout his career Monty had always categorically stated that he'd never play on the Champions Tour. However, the large prize money, the desire to win in America, and to win a Major, even a Champions Tour major, caused a change of mind so he joined the Champions Tour in 2013 making ten starts without success.

Then in 2014, three weeks after Jimenez' Champions Tour win which must have inspired him, Monty secured his first ever victory in the USA, and his first ever Major triumph when he easily won the USPGA Seniors Championship at Harbour Shores in Michigan by four shots. He then went on to win the US Seniors' Open so by mid-July he'd won two of the three senior Majors!

As Derek Lawrenson asked in the Daily Mail 'Did someone switch off that notorious temper once he reached 50? Did he finally realise you can't pick a fight with American galleries and still win a major?'

Yes he had the advantage of playing against players older than himself nevertheless Derek was surely correct when he said what had happened was that passing the big five-O had made the difference as we saw a calmer, more relaxed, and controlled player who was allowing his massive talent to freely express itself.

As we'll see later in Chapter 7 on Inspiration by Comparison the timing of Monty's first Champions Tour win was probably linked to Jimenez' Champions Tour win on his first Champions Tour start just weeks earlier.

ASSESSMENT

Landmark birthdays can be very important in all our lives and certainly in the lives of professional sportsmen with their potency based mainly on THREE key effects.

First, when in the Nines with a Landmark birthday looming on the horizon the process of personal re-assessment often starts.

Second, once the Landmark birthday has been passed there can be a feeling of release creating renewed energy, fresh drive and new goals.

Third, a Landmark birthday can provide the target date by which time you aim to achieve a particular target or a particular victory.

Of course there will be those who simply carry on with their sporting career without paying too much attention to birthdays. However, as the many examples we have used show, I suspect that the majority of sportsmen like the rest of us, are very heavily influenced by the approach and then the passing of Landmark birthdays.

We have so far seen the importance of births with the Nappy Factor, and the impact of landmark birthdays so having looked at births and birthdays we now move on from the start of life and the annual celebrations of that birth to the end of life as we examine the effects of death as a motivating factor.

CHAPTER FOUR
THE FUNERAL FACTOR

WHAT IS THE FUNERAL FACTOR?

We have just seen how births and the onset of Landmark birthdays can give sportsmen a real extra incentive to improve performance and now we move from the effects of births and birthdays at the start of life to the end of life, to the impact that death and bereavement can have.

So let's examine what I have called the Funeral Factor as we look at the way in which bereavement can also act as a motivating force that can enhance sporting performance. We will see that there is definite evidence that although this Funeral Factor is extremely powerful in the short term it can also have a long term impact.

Let's look at its potency in FOUR different sports — Football, American football, Snooker and Golf.

FOOTBALL

Here we have FIVE very different examples of the motivational effect of the Funeral Factor

2014 World Cup — Chile inspired by the Copiaco mining accident

Chile had been drawn in Group B with Australia, Spain and Holland and with those two strong European countries the finalists in the 2010 World Cup it was expected that Chile would be eliminated as they were said to be in a 'Group of Death'.

In Chile you may well recall the Copiaco mining accident of 2010 when 33 miners were trapped underground for 69 days before they were all rescued alive and in the main uninjured with their rescue shown globally on TV and YouTube. Initially it had been thought that all the miners would be killed so their dramatic successful escape was placed at the heart of a motivational TV advert in Chile before the 2014 World Cup which said that, 'Nothing is impossible for a Chilean, the Group of Death doesn't scare us. We've already beaten it.' In other words that mine rescue when 33 Chileans survived when they were expected to die was being used as proof that as Chileans had already beaten real death then 'death' in a football sense could also be defeated.

To add to the motivational impact of the Mining analogy dirt from that mine was scattered on Chile's training pitch before the tournament started. The motivation worked as Chile were impressive especially as they played as a real 'band of brothers', a united team playing for each other without any selfish egos. They beat Australia 3-2, and then the World Cup holders Spain 2-0 so they had survived 'the Group of Death' and qualified for the round of the last 16 in which they faced the hosts Brazil and they played superbly in a 1-1 draw before after extra time they lost on penalties. Chile had lost yet they were a genuine team, an inspired team and one in which their country, and its miners, could take great pride.

Clearly in this context there were no funerals so here we see the successful use of a highly publicised collective near-death experience as a powerful motivational tool for a national team.

2014: The Funeral Factor works its motivational magic in Bristol

When Bristol City played at home to Gillingham in a League One fixture on 1st March 2014 it was set to be an 'ordinary' game although an important one especially for the home side, who were relegated from the Championship the previous season, and were 4th from bottom of the league table staring a second successive relegation in the face. They had won only 5 of their previous 18 home league matches whereas Gillingham by contrast were in a much more comfortable 13th place.

However, there wasn't to be the usual pre match team talk before this game as the club had agreed that lifelong fan, father of three, 54-year-old Mark Saunders who had been given only days to live could address the team. He told the players they were privileged people and he reminded them of how their mums and dads had spent time on wet evenings taking them to train so they could follow their dreams, 'you should remember how lucky you are,' and he stressed that it was time for them to give something back to the fans as they had been so poor this season. Mark's brother Bill said afterwards that the team listened in stunned silence before as Mark finished there was spontaneous applause. I'm sure you can guess the rest ... Bristol City gave their best performance of the season winning 2-1 and so they moved out of the relegation places. There can be no doubt that the Funeral Factor worked that afternoon in that dressing room and it continued to work as City then won their next two games, both away matches. Indeed after that inspirational speech City won 14 points from a W-W-W-D-D-W sequence in their next six games and went on to stay well clear of relegation finishing the season in a comfortable 12th place.

2013: Arsenal v Southampton

In this Premier League fixture in November Olivier Giroud was man of the match for Arsenal who won 2-0 with the French striker scoring both the Gunners' two goals. However, 'two days before the match I lost my grandfather. So I was really motivated, and I hope he is proud of me in the sky. It was a pleasure to score and I want to dedicate the goals to him.'

1996: Matthew Harding and Chelsea FC

Matthew had built a huge personal fortune in the insurance industry, and in 1994 with Chelsea's finances in serious trouble he put many millions into his beloved club in exchange for a seat on the board. Over the next couple of years he and Chairman Ken Bates often publicly disagreed with Harding being seen as 'The Peoples' Champion'. So when he died on 22nd October 1996 in a tragic helicopter crash flying home after seeing Chelsea lose in a League Cup tie at Bolton his death shocked and saddened both Chelsea fans and indeed Chelsea players.

Four days later with emotions still raw Chelsea were at home in an important league match to London rivals Tottenham Hotspur. No surprise then that Chelsea in a red-hot atmosphere won 3-1. Later that season Chelsea went on to lift the FA Cup at Wembley beating Middlesbrough 2-0 with that win dedicated to Matthew's memory.

That season the North Stand at Stamford Bridge was named the Matthew Harding Stand.

15th April 1989: FA Cup semi-final. Liverpool v Nottingham Forest and the Hillsborough Disaster

As a result of this day 96 Liverpool fans died in a tragedy that will never be forgotten in Liverpool or by the club's fans. The FA Cup match against Nottingham Forest was stopped when still goalless after just six minutes. As the full horrors of that day became known the city went into mourning and Liverpool didn't play another game that month.

It was eventually decided that the FA Cup should continue. So after a time when so many players and club staff had attended the funerals Liverpool met Nottingham Forest in the rescheduled game at Old Trafford on May 7th. Against such an emotional background and with such huge support there could only be one winner of that semi-final so it was no surprise that Liverpool beat Forest 3-1. Steve Staunton, the youngest Liverpool player on the field at Hillsborough, said after the Old Trafford win: 'Talk about having to win a game. I felt it more strongly against Forest than any other match before or since.' Liverpool went on to lift the FA Cup beating local rivals Everton 3-2 after extra time in the Wembley final in a match, and on a day, I'll never forget.

20th April 2014: Five days after the 25th anniversary of the Hillsborough Disaster, Norwich v Liverpool in the Premier League

This game was played five days after the 25th anniversary of Hillsborough, and on that anniversary day at Anfield, in front of 25,000, Margaret Aspinall, the Chair of the Hillsborough Families Support Group had said that, 'Stress is difficult but stress is also good, it gives you the determination to fight on'. So Liverpool manager Brendan Rodgers, understanding the motivational power that Hillsborough can have, decided to stick those words on the dressing room wall as inspiration before the game at Norwich which, at the end of a very emotional week, Liverpool won 3-2.

AMERICAN FOOTBALL
Some of the strongest examples of the Funeral Factor at work, both on an

individual and on a team, are to be found in the ultra-tough, ultra-macho world of American football in the NFL.

2003: Brett Favre — the legendary quarterback of the Green Bay packers

On the evening of Sunday 21st Dec 2003 Brett's father Irvin died after a heart attack while driving. His death was both totally unexpected and totally shocking.

'My dad had been with me to every game from 5th grade and he coached me in high school,' and as Brett and his dad had been extremely close the news must have had a devastating effect on the star quarterback.

The immediate decision for Brett was whether he should play the very next evening in the televised game against the Oakland Raiders, and Brett was clear as, 'I knew that my dad would have wanted me to play.' So after addressing all his team-mates and coaches at a meeting when you could hear a pin drop he played and I'm sure you can guess the rest!

Brett gave one of the best-ever performances of his 13-year career as he passed for 399 yards and 4 touchdowns as the Packers beat the Raiders 41-7.

Brett's decision to play had also inspired the whole team as tight-end Wesley Wells admitted that, 'I think it's fair to say that we were all inspired.'

However, in all professional sport, as in life, the fear of failure can be very strong so to decide to play was one thing but then to play to such a high standard showed how powerful the Funeral Factor can be as a potent motivating force that blocks out any negativity or fear of failure. Wide receiver Antonio Freeman summed up the thoughts of Brett's team-mates when he said, 'What he had to deal with today was immeasurable...I don't know how he did it.'

Within two years the Funeral Factor inspired two bereaved players in the same NFL team to play on and win.

2011: Ed Reed — The Pro Bowl safety for the Baltimore Ravens

In January 2011 Ed Reed's brother Brian was reported missing presumed drowned in the Mississippi river two days before the massively important AFC wildcard game against Kansas City. Ed was a key player for the Ravens shown by the fact that since he started to play in the NFL he had made more interceptions [54] than any other player.

Ed, like Brett Favre eight years earlier, decided to play and again, you've guessed it, Ed made 4 tackles in a 30-7 win. As coach John Harbaugh said, 'For Ed to do what he did under the circumstances and to play the way he played, to lead the way he led, that's just an incredible thing...I think what Ed's going through, what the Reed family is going through, is a big part of the victory'. The Ravens' legendary linebacker Ray Lewis summed up the team bonding impact that the Funeral Factor had had when he said, 'Anytime you lose someone like that it just draws every one of us closer.'

2012: Torrey Smith — the Baltimore Ravens' wide receiver

On 23rd September 2012 the Baltimore Ravens' wide receiver Torrey Smith learned that his 19-year-old brother had died in a motorcycle accident. Smith left the team hotel to be with his family knowing that the next evening the Ravens had a vital NFL game against the New England Patriots. Coach John Harbaugh left Torrey to decide whether he would play and play he did as he starred with 6 receptions for 127 yards and two touchdowns to help his team overcome an early 13-0 deficit to go on to win, in the last minute, 31-30. After his first touchdown Smith went down on one knee pointed to the sky and said a quick prayer and his inspired performance led teammate and running back Ray Rice afterwards to say 'what a show he put on for a brother tonight.'

Please note that in the next chapter on 'The God Squad', we will return to Torrey Smith and Ed Reed as their very strong religious beliefs were central to the way they handled their bereavements.

We have just seen how the Funeral Factor can inspire players in two team sports, Football and American football, in games that are completed in a single day. However, there are also many examples of the amazing impact that bereavement can have in individual sports that are played over many days so they provide the perfect test to see if the Funeral Factor can maintain an impact over a length of time.

So let's look at EIGHT examples spread over more than 20 years from Golf and a very recent one in Snooker.

GOLF

1995: Ben Crenshaw's emotional win in the 1995 US Masters

Almost 20 years ago there was a really poignant example in a world class tournament in front of a worldwide audience that was to confirm the immense motivating power that bereavement can unleash.

Crenshaw had already won a coveted Green Jacket when winning the US Masters in 1984 however, eleven years later he was in poor form. Prior to Augusta he had missed the cut in three of his previous four tournaments, hadn't shot a round in the 60s in two months, and even his legendary brilliance on the greens had largely disappeared as he was ranked only 59th for putting.

However, Ben's mind wasn't on Augusta in the week of the 1995 US Masters as he flew 850 miles to be at the funeral of 90-year-old Harvey Penick as it was Harvey who'd first put a golf club into Ben's six year old hands and who'd been Ben's only coach throughout his career. Ben had been a pallbearer at the funeral before flying back to Augusta on

Wednesday feeling tired, drained, and with a sore foot that he thought might require surgery.

However, his wife Julie observed that, 'There was this calmness to him all week that I have never seen before,' and Ben himself said, 'it was kind of like I felt this hand on my shoulder guiding me along.'

Ben got the breaks when he needed them to win by a single shot from Davis Love. As the final putt went in Ben collapsed in tears, while the bookies collapsed in laughter, at the success of a 66/1 out of form 'no hoper'. Ben himself said 'I don't think I ever had a quicker transformation' so it was clear that bereavement had had a massive positive effect on the then 43-year-old American.

2006: The Open becomes the first and so far only double Funeral Factor Major

Tiger Wood's dad died on 3rd May 2006 and after a nine week absence a 'very rusty' Tiger returned to play in the US Open when he missed his first ever major cut. However, after that his form figs were an astonishing 2-W-W-W-W-W-W-W!!

After the US Open failure he won both the year's final majors The Open and the USPGA, and the year's final two World Golf Championships.

'My dad was my best friend and greatest role model and I will miss him deeply'. So was Tiger's amazing form in the second half of 2006 inspired by the Funeral Factor? Of course he was at that time a truly superb golfer whose performance levels were always high because he was always so ambitious, determined and focused. However, even in his case I do think that Tiger was inspired by the Funeral Factor, especially when he won the 2006 Open after all, although it was his 11th Major win, it was the first since he stood by his dad's grave two months earlier. As his final putt dropped his imprisoned emotions escaped as he cried uncontrollably in the arms of his caddie, Steve Williams and then as he hugged his wife Elin. Clearly he had his father very much on his mind as he said 'I wish he would have seen it [his win] one more time.'

> However, the really remarkable thing about that tournament at the Royal Liverpool golf club was that it was the only time when the Funeral Factor affected both the leading contenders.

American Chris DiMarco's mother had died from cancer just three weeks earlier so Chris insisted on bringing his dad over to The Open as he was determined to honour his mum's memory by playing well although he'd been in poor recent form. Indeed since March 1st he'd missed 7 of 13 cuts and posted just one top 30 finish. However, inspired by the Funeral Factor he pushed Tiger all the way before losing by just two strokes. 'I had my mother with me all week,' he said after finishing second in a major for the third time, and each time it had been Tiger who had beaten him!

2006: Ryder Cup held at the K Club in County Kildare, Ireland

This was the Ryder Cup that will be remembered for many reasons such as the two teams partying together after it ended, yet it will always be remembered as Darren Clarke's Ryder Cup.

On August 12th Darren's wife died, after losing her battle with breast cancer, so less than six weeks later, it was a very emotional moment when Darren stepped onto the first tee in front of his home fans in the final four-ball match on the first morning playing with Lee Westwood against Phil Mickelson and Chris DiMarco. The Funeral Factor was clearly at work as Darren and Lee won that match by 1 hole, and then again with Lee Westwood they beat Tiger Woods and Jim Furyk by 3 and 2 in the second day's fourballs. Finally on Sunday Darren beat Zach Johnson 3 and 2 in the singles so he had won all his three matches as Europe easily retained the Ryder Cup winning by 18.5 pts to 9.5 pts.

Captain Ian Woosnam's side had the better players in better form, and in bad weather on a course they knew so well they were always going to win. Nevertheless the Funeral Factor had been at work throughout and it showed both in Darren's unbeaten performance and in the determination of the other members of the European Team to win especially for him.

2013: Ryan Palmer's superb performance in the Players' Championship after the sudden shocking death of his best friend

36-year-old American golfer Ryan Palmer was playing in the Players' Championship on the famous Sawgrass course in Florida when he received the shocking, indeed horrendous news that his lifelong very close friend Clay Anderholt had been killed in a freak road accident in Ryan's home state of Texas. He had just shot 67 in his opening round however, after speaking to his wife Jennifer, and his sports psychologist Fran Pirozzolo and considering the difficulty of getting to Texas which was 1,000 miles away Ryan decided to play on.

He went on to play extremely well to be just two shots off the lead with three holes to play. He finished tied 5th which would have been a superb performance at any time. It was surely an inspired performance especially when we remember that Ryan had previously missed the cut on six of his previous seven starts on the tricky Sawgrass course with his best ever finish 75th,and his average score 74! After his last putt on the final hole he covered his face with his cap as the emotions flooded out. Later he flew home to be a pallbearer at his buddy's funeral.

2013: 'It was a great way to punch home what my Mum meant to me' — golfer Justin Walters

32-year-old South African golfer Justin Walters' mum was suffering from cancer when he earned his card for the 2013 European Tour season. At the start of that year especially with some tournaments in his own country he played OK with three top 20 finishes as he made 6 cuts in 8 starts.

However, from April his form worsened rapidly as he was visiting his mum on Mondays and Tuesdays before then flying to whichever tournament course he was playing on. 'I lost a bit of drive and a bit of focus,' and so he missed 6 successive cuts, and overall he missed 12 cuts in 16 tournaments from April until his mum died in September.

In the first event after her death he was 26th in the Dunhill Links and so moved to 126th in the Race to Dubai. He therefore needed a high finish in the next event The Portugal Masters to retain his tour card for 2014.' I had the mind-set that it didn't matter if I played well or if I played badly as my aim was to honour my mum', and although a rank outsider at 250/1, that was exactly what Justin did especially with a superb second round 63. With the final round to play he was 4 shots off the lead in T9th place so he was in contention to win the event. However, although that chance had gone when he stood on the tee at the final hole he knew that a par would be enough for him to finish 2nd and so keep his Tour card. However, that chance looked remote when he faced a 50 foot putt across that last green for that par 4. Again, you've guessed it ... he rammed the ball into the hole and then with his hands covering his face he cried, and cried and cried!!

'I felt the whole world lift off me ... it was a great way to punch home what my Mum meant to me'.

Last year in 2014 there were FOUR more examples of the Funeral Factor at work — one in snooker, two in golf, and one in December in cricket.

SNOOKER
May 2014: Mark Selby beats Ronnie O'Sullivan to win the World Championship

After Mark Selby had won the title for the first time and when clearly filled with emotion he immediately dedicated his win to his Dad, who had died from cancer in 1999 just a couple of months before Mark, then a 16-year-old, turned pro. He recalled his final conversation with his Dad, 'his last words to me were I want you to become World Champion. I said I would, that it was just when not if.' Inspired by a steely determination to fulfil that promise to his Dad Mark, the 'Jester from Leicester', had won 13 of the last 17 frames to beat a truly great defending Champion in Ronnie O'Sullivan.

Later he also dedicated his win to Malcolm Thorne, elder brother of TV commentator Willie, who had died of cancer three years ago as, 'Malcolm was the one who spotted me and sponsored me for a few years. He took me under his wing and it all happened from there.'

GOLF
July 2014: George McNeil's final round 61 on the day his sister died

George decided to play the Greenbrier Classic even though he had withdrawn from the following week's tournament to be with his family as his sister Michelle was seriously ill with cancer. However, before playing his final round on Sunday George had been told that his sister Michelle's battle with cancer was very nearly over. His mom had told him 'it might be in the next couple of minutes, the next couple of hours, but it's going to happen soon'.

George then went out to play a truly amazing round of golf as he was 6 under par, including a hole in one, after just 8 holes on his way to posting a 9 under par round of 61 in which he putted brilliantly and hit 16 of the 18 greens. It was a round that saw him rocket up the leader board to finish second. However, during his round his sister had died, and, 'then when I finished I talked to my mom and she told me.'

Surely it was no coincidence that he played that brilliant round on the day he knew his sister had so little time left.

September 2014. The final words the European players saw before they went out to play in and win the Ryder Cup.

The words were 'Happiest days of your lives'. They were the words that the hugely popular golf coach Bob Torrance would say to his players after they left the driving range to walk to the first tee. The European captain Paul McGinley with his superb attention to detail ensured that as his players went out to play they would be inspired by the words and memory of a lovely man who had died just two months earlier.

CRICKET
December 2014.'The little man up there was with me and it all fell into place.'

On November 25th Australian test batsman Phillip Hughes was 63 not out when he suffered a 'catastrophic' injury after he was struck on the head by a bouncer when playing in a Sheffield Shield match against New South Wales He never regained consciousness and died two days later after which the stunned worldwide cricketing family fell into a state of shock.

However, exactly two weeks after that tragic incident it was decided that the first test at the Adelaide Oval against India should go ahead. Australian batsman David Warner had been a close friend of Phillip as together they had opened the batting in many innings. So when that first test started with Australia batting first Warner wanted to honour his close friend and batting superbly he did just that. In the first innings when he reached 50 he 'looked to the heavens', on 63 Hughes' score when he was injured, he dropped to his knees, and when he reached his century David Warner leapt high into the Adelaide air. After that century he said that 'the little man up there was with me and it all fell into place...the hardest part of the day for me was when I was on 63'.Still inspired he scored 102 in the second innings and so played a key role in Australia's 48 run victory.

There will be those who'll talk of fate, destiny and that it was meant to be.

However, there can surely be little doubt that David Warner's two centuries and Australia's victory were classic examples of the Funeral Factor at work.

THE UNIQUE CASE OF JUSTIN ROSE AND THE FUNERAL FACTOR
2002
Golfer Justin Rose's dad Ken had been Justin's coach and, 'my relationship with my dad was the best it could be, he is why I play the game.' Under his dad's guidance Justin had built a first class amateur career highlighted in 1997 when he was the second youngest ever player to play in the Walker Cup, which is the amateurs Ryder Cup. A year later he burst onto the big stage when he famously chipped in at the final hole in the Open at Royal Birkdale to finish tied 4th and win the silver medal as the top amateur.

He then turned pro the next day and faced the ultimate test of character as he missed the cut in his first 21, yes 21, tournaments!! However, he never got down on himself and with his father's encouragement he slowly and patiently improved. In 2001 he finished 2nd twice in South Africa and he posted two other top ten finishes.

In 2002 it became clear that his dad Ken, who had been suffering from leukaemia, 'was not going to make it' and he died in September of that year. In our earlier examples we have seen that there can be a positive impact shortly after the death of a loved one, however, in the case of Justin the impact of his dad's illness was much earlier. Put simply he knew he just had to win while his dad was still alive. So 2002 was to become a very special and successful year for the 31-year-old Johannesburg-born Justin — 'I had to show him I could do it,' and that's precisely what he did.

Justin posted his maiden victory on the European Tour when he won the Alfred Dunhill Championship in South Africa in January, he then won the Nashua Masters on South Africa's Sunshine Tour and the Crowns Tournament on the Japanese Tour — three wins on three different tours within three months!! However, his dad's illness had prevented him from seeing any of those successes. That was to change in June at Woburn in the Victor Chandler British Masters.

Justin after being 6 shots off the lead at halfway played superbly over the final two weekend rounds to win by a single shot with his sick dad watching. It was to be a very special moment as it was the first and sadly the only time that Ken saw Justin win a professional tournament.

Within three months of seeing his son's win Ken finally lost his battle with cancer. Although he won four times in 2002, after his dad's funeral Justin went four years without another win until he won the Australian Masters in November 2006, and in 2007 he won twice so finishing 1st on the European Order of Merit.

In Justin's case it was as if the Funeral Factor was brought forward so the effect of his dad's ill health had a strong motivating effect on him while his dad was seriously ill rather than straight after his death.

We have seen many examples of the impact of bereavement yet here we have the impact of the period before bereavement rather than of the period after it.

2013. The inspirational impact of a bereavement in the case of Justin Rose took over a decade to have its biggest impact

Justin's success in winning the 2007 Order of Merit led to him moving to Florida where his first child, a son, was born in 2009 and in 2010, his Nappy Factor year, he won for the first time on American soil when winning the prestigious Memorial Tournament and then following it up with a further win in the AT+T.

With his second child, a daughter born in 2012, and his first win in a World Golf Championship [WGC] at Doral in 2011, Justin had with his wins in America won on all the world's golf tours, he'd won a WGC so only a Major golf tournament was missing from his CV.

13th June was the final day of the 2013 US Open, it was also Father's Day in America, and it was to be the day Justin made history!

Through the first three rounds Justin had played with a calm patience sticking to his game plan so as Father's Day dawned with one round to play he was tied 5th two shots behind Phil Mickelson, the tournament leader and the favourite with both the galleries and the bookies. On the eve of the final round his coach Sean Foley sent Justin one of the best ever motivational messages when he said 'Go out and be the man your Dad would be proud of, and the man your kids can look up to'. That was so skilfully constructed as it brought together three generations referring as it did to Justin's dad, to Justin himself and to Justin's children.

Cool, calm and patient throughout Justin stood on the tee at the final hole knowing that, almost certainly, to win he needed to make a par on that ultra-tough par 4 hole. He did just that and immediately pointed his index finger to the skies and as he admitted later he inwardly said, 'Dad, I gave it everything today. That was for you.' The significance of Father's Day had been ever present that day in Justin's mind. It was one tremendous achievement as he became the first English Major winner for 17 years and the first British player to win the US Open for 43 years!!

So the Justin and Ken Rose story relates to the Funeral Factor in three very interesting if unusual ways

1. In 2002 we saw a pre-bereavement positive impact on Justin's game.

2. For the first four years without his Dad Justin didn't win and a contributory factor may well have been that mentally he was re-adjusting to life without his dad.

3. Over a decade after his dad died the Funeral Factor played a really significant part in an historic golfing achievement when Justin won the 2013 US Open.

ASSESSING THE FUNERAL FACTOR
Its origin
The realisation that bereavement could act as a major motivating factor was born in my mind after the appalling Hillsborough Tragedy when on May 7th 1989 the rescheduled FA Cup semi-final between Liverpool and Nottingham Forest was played at Old Trafford. There was absolutely no way that I could see any result other than a Liverpool win and so it proved when the Reds won 3-1.

I first wrote about the Funeral Factor in 1995 by which time the golfing example of Ben Crenshaw in that year had shown how powerful the immediate effect of bereavement could be, and as we have seen there have been plenty of examples since then in both individual and team sports including that recent December 2014 cricketing example.

IS IT IN BAD TASTE TO DISCUSS THE SPORTING EFFECTS OF DEATH?
I would suggest that today death has become the one subject about which we seem to have a social taboo shown by the very odd euphemistic language we tend to use. For example we hardly ever refer to someone's death as we prefer alternatives such as 'someone had passed away', 'moved on', or 'is no longer with us'. However, my favourite is when we are said to have 'lost' someone as in 'he lost his wife', 'she lost her son', and 'she lost her husband'. Sorry but you don't lose your wife you lose your car keys …. you don't lose your son you lose your glasses … you don't lose your husband you lose your credit card!

I think our unwillingness to use the word death, our reluctance often to even discuss the subject, and our refusal often even to say that someone has died is both interesting and sad especially when we all know that death is the one thing we all have in common. So there will be those who have a feeling of discomfort when the Funeral Factor rears its head.

Perhaps the softer term 'The Bereavement Factor' would be more acceptable, but sorry I'm sticking with the alliterative and so more memorable Funeral Factor.

THE FUNERAL FACTOR IN ACTION
There are FOUR ways in which the Funeral Factor can have a motivating impact.

1. There can be a pre-bereavement impact as a sportsman strives for success while the loved one is still alive and able to enjoy the success.

2. After the bereavement the strongly felt emotions enable the Funeral Factor to have an impact in the short term.

3. It is possible that even many years after the death that the Funeral Factor can, in rare cases, still have a potent effect.

4. We have also seen in the Chilean example how motivational messages relating to near-death experience can be successfully used.

DOES IT ALWAYS WORK?

We have already stressed with the Nappy Factor and Landmark birthdays that although these factors can act as powerful motivators for professional sportsmen they are not universally applicable and the same applies to the Funeral Factor.

Of course there will be examples of bereaved sportsmen whose form may not improve at all after a bereavement. Indeed the opposite may well be true as in the case of 24-year-old Thai golfer Kiradech Aphibarnrat, whose long-term coach Natpasit Chokthanasart died in December 2013. 'Since I lost my coach my mental approach has been different, I have lost some confidence,' and it showed big style as the popular 'go for it' Thai player had form figures of Missed Cut-67-64-67 in his first four stroke play events of 2014. It wasn't until the Indonesian Masters in late April, having worked with a new coach, that he regained his form when 4th in the Indonesian Masters.

The effect of any bereavement will therefore depend on the particular individual circumstances nevertheless we have seen enough evidence to suggest that there can be dramatic positive motivational effects before a bereavement, and in both the short and long term following a death.

One press criticism when I introduced the Funeral Factor was that it was 'far-fetched and morbid'.

IS IT FAR-FETCHED?

Well the examples in both team and individual sports in this chapter show conclusively that it's most definitely not far-fetched as it can be a really potent influence on sporting performance. So the 'far-fetched' criticism seems really superficial and in fact it is itself actually rather 'far-fetched!'

IS IT MORBID?

Well 'morbid' is defined as 'an unusual interest in death' yet the Funeral Factor is NOT about death as such as it's about the effects of death, and that is a subtle yet very significant and very important difference. So in a real sense it's not about the death it's actually about how the living who were very close to the deceased can become highly motivated when they become or are about to become bereaved.

IS IT MORALLY WRONG TO HAVE A BET HAVING USED THE FUNERAL FACTOR IN YOUR ANALYSIS?

It could be said that if you have a bet after using the Funeral Factor in sports analysis you are trying to profit from someone's death. This would seem to be an extremely harsh view to take. After all if, for example, you study a football match and see that one side has several players injured with say broken legs, fractured ankles, dislocated shoulders, and then back their opponents who are at full strength can it really be said that you are trying to profit from the injuries of the players? Surely you are making a judgment of the likely winners using the available information and that is therefore acceptable.

It seems to me reasonable when assessing a sporting event to assess ALL the factors that may impact on performance and sometimes if that results in analysing the impact of a bereavement that seems fair, logical and sensible.

If you feel uncomfortable should the Funeral Factor lead you to a winning wager as often it will then I suggest that you donate your winnings to your favourite charity or, better still, donate it to the favourite charity of the deceased.

FINALLY DEATH AND RELIGION

We have already noted that the language used regarding bereavements can be euphemistic. Indeed an alternative way of saying that someone has died is to say they have 'passed on' or 'moved on' or 'are no longer with us' with the clear implication that they have moved to another place such as heaven or paradise where eventually we will meet them again.

You will have noticed that in several of our examples there is reference by those bereaved to God, divine intervention and to an afterlife, so it is to the effect that religious belief has on sporting achievement that we now turn in the next chapter on 'The God Squad'.

CHAPTER FIVE
THE GOD SQUAD

In recent years it has become increasingly obvious that religion plays a very significant part in the lives of many sportsmen.

You only have to watch any English Premier League football match, or indeed in many of the 2014 World Cup games to see players as the teams run on to the pitch crossing themselves, pointing to the 'heavens' or kissing the ground to realise that religious faith is very important to many top-class footballers.

To help in the analysis of this issue we can probably divide sportsmen into four distinct categories.

First there are those who simply do not have any religious belief at all.

They simply do not believe there is any form of deity and do not accept that there is a life after death. They may well have disowned the beliefs they were brought up in and now they may be active Humanists who are members of the British Association of Humanists, or they may simply live their lives without being part of any organisation.

It may well be that the reluctance of many England footballers to sing the National Anthem before an International match is because to sing 'God Save The Queen' with honesty, passion and integrity you have to believe in both God and the Monarchy and I suspect several players simply don't believe in either God or the Monarchy, or maybe both. It is therefore rather unfair to criticise the players for being unpatriotic when they don't wholeheartedly sing the National Anthem.

Regarding religious faith sportsmen and women probably fall into three groups.

First there are those who have maintained the faith they were brought up in although those inherited views now play a minimal role in their lives.

So yes if they were brought up as Christians they will attend Christian Funerals and Christenings but they do not attend Church and spend little if any time, thinking about religion. So any sporting success or failure they may have cannot be linked to their inherited, inactive, and so inconsequential religious faith.

The second group have religious beliefs which, although they play a significant role in their daily lives, they tend to keep them to themselves.

So this group are comfortable to be known as Christians, Muslims, Buddhists, Hindus or Jews because regular prayers and regular visits to their places of worship are a regular part of their lives. Nevertheless they tend to keep their sporting and religious lives separate, and so would not discuss their religious views with the media. Nevertheless their privately held religious beliefs may contribute to their sporting success although they would not publicly discuss any link between their faith and their sports success.

As we will see later in this chapter, the former Manchester United manager David Moyes is a Christian who falls into this category.

The God Squad is the third group. They have deeply held beliefs that play a major role in their lives and they are very willing to be seen to publicly link their faith to their sporting results.

Here we find that there is a willingness to publicly speak about their religious beliefs and how those beliefs enable them to develop, improve and win as professional sportsmen.

I've selected God Squad examples from TWO individual sports, Boxing and Golf, and TWO from team sports, Football and American football [NFL].

Boxing: Muhammad Ali says 'I talk to God every day' immediately after becoming the Heavyweight Champion of the World

One of the earliest examples of a successful sportsman in the God Squad group was Cassius Clay who was to change his name to Mohammed Ali, the name by which this legendary heavyweight Champion of the World became known.

He first became interested in spiritual matters as a 17-year-old amateur boxer when he learned about The Nation of Islam [NOI]. He attended his first NOI meeting a couple of years later and in 1962 he first met its leader Malcolm X. The importance of the Nation of Islam to him was shown when several of its well-known members, including Malcolm X himself, attended his big fight for the Heavyweight Championship of the World against Sonny Liston in 1964.

That fight was the defining moment in Ali's career. Up to that point he had won an Olympic Heavyweight gold medal, was undefeated as a pro, while his opponent Sonny Liston was a fearsome fighter with a criminal record and alleged links to 'The Mob' so Liston was a long odds on favourite regarded by all the boxing experts as a certainty to win and so silence the ultra-cocky Cassius Clay.

Liston's defeat was one of the great sporting shocks of all time and in a famous interview in the ring immediately after the fight the new World Champion showed how essential, important and central his faith was to him when he revealed that 'I talk to God every day'. For him to immediately think of God at a time of such massive personal excitement showed beyond doubt how important his faith was to him. Shortly after that fight he formally joined the Nation of Islam and changed his name so Cassius Clay became Muhammad Ali, and the rest is history! The name he had taken for religious reasons was to become one of the most famous sporting names of all time.

AMERICAN FOOTBALL
2012: When the God Squad met the Funeral Factor — Ed Reed and Torrey Smith

You'll recall that in the last chapter we had the stories of two American football stars, Ed Reed and Torrey Smith, who both played for the Baltimore Ravens, and who both played a big NFL game immediately after the death of a brother, and who both starred as their team won the game. Both players, and the Ravens team itself, were inspired by the Funeral Factor with their Christian religion also playing a very important role in their success.

You'll recall that wide receiver Torrey Smith scored two key touchdowns in the 31-30 last minute win by the Ravens over the Patriots in September 2012. Before that game Ed Reed who, twenty months earlier, had played straight after his brother's death gave Torrey Smith a psalm that he thought would help Torrey through that tough time. Ed also said that 'I still talk to my brother every day because I know there's much more to us than just being here...I just know he's in a much better place'. Before the game Smith had prayed and after his first touchdown he went down on one knee pointed to the sky and 'I said a quick prayer.'

Reading through the stories of those two players there can be absolutely no doubt at all that religious faith was of crucial importance when Ed Reed and Torrey Smith played on after a brother's death. Indeed as we'll now see it was absolutely central to the Ravens winning the Super Bowl which is the biggest prize In American Sport.

February 2013: Ray Lewis and the Baltimore Ravens win Superbowl XLVII — Isaiah 54:17.

Ray Lewis, the Ravens legendary linebacker, in the 2012-13 NFL season provided one of the best ever examples of a sporting leader with immense motivational powers that were based on an unshakeable Christian belief in God and Heaven. He went to the Bible to Isaiah 54:17 and took the quote 'No Weapon formed against you shall prosper' and shortened it to 'No Weapon', and used that phrase and gave those two words the meaning that no opponent, no venue, no individual, no circumstance, no climatic element, no opposing crowd could possibly stop them. 'No Weapon' also took on another meaning because as it was Ray Lewis' last season the belief was that it was fate or destiny for the Ravens to succeed and that was the reason 'No Weapon' would ever succeed against them.

The Ravens' head coach John Harbaugh was convinced that 'God and heaven work in mysterious, wonderful ways' so mirroring the beliefs of Ray Lewis who would often say that 'God is amazing' after games as the Ravens successful season gathered pace. The 'No Weapon' mantra was very much in evidence on January 12th 2013 when in the AFC Divisional Final the Ravens met the Denver Broncos, who were on an eleven game unbeaten run, in a game to be played in Denver at their Mile High Stadium. The Broncos were the favourites to win, but in a pulsating close encounter the Ravens tied the game with 30 seconds to go and went on to win 38-35 in overtime. That win confirmed their belief that they were destined to win the Super Bowl after all 'No Weapon', not even a tough away game against opponents on a hot winning streak, could stop them!

They went on to beat the Patriots 28-13, and then they met the 49ers in the Super Bowl final in New Orleans. There was one very interesting, if unusual, moment in that final when the electricity failed and the lights went out in half the Stadium when head coach John Harbaugh walked up to Ray Lewis and said...[yes, you've guessed it] 'No Weapon!' Not even a power failure was going to prevent them from reaching their destiny. Before a TV audience of over 108 million the Ravens won 34-31 — helped by the power of Isaiah 54:17.

FOOTBALL

The following are FIVE examples of the importance of religion in the 2014 World Cup the final of which was played in Rio de Janeiro, the city overlooked by the massive sculpture of Christ the Redeemer.

2014 World Cup: After England's first goal its scorer mouths 'I love you Jesus and praise you for everything'

After Liverpool striker Daniel Sturridge scored England's goal in their first Group match against Italy he did his usual special celebratory arm-waving dance. However, more significantly he also showed that his religious faith was very important to him as he looked up to the skies with arms raised with pointed fingers and his words, noted by lip readers, were 'I love you Jesus, and I praise you for everything.' That equalising goal was so important to England that in the uncontrolled celebrations that followed the long serving physiotherapist Gary Lewin dislocated his ankle and had to return home yet its scorer had the self-control to spend some time remembering the central importance of his faith to him.

2014 World Cup: England's SAS are in the God Squad

Sturridge's fellow Liverpool forward 19-year-old Raheem Sterling is also a devout Christian having been brought up to go to Church in Jamaica by his mum Nadine. So England's two fastest players Sturridge and Sterling, called the SAS by the press, are definitely members of the God Squad, and it's clear that like many top flight footballers today their religious faith is extremely important to them

2014 World Cup: 50/1 shock Group winners Costa Rica pray after reaching the last sixteen

Before the World Cup started Costa Rica were the rank outsiders at 4000/1 to lift the Jules Rimet trophy, and 50/1 even to win Group D. However, the no hopers beat Uruguay 3-1 in their opening match, and then shocked Italy beating them 1-0. After that superb victory the Costa Rican players knew they had qualified for a place in the last sixteen so they stayed locked in their dressing room for 45 minutes reportedly to pray giving thanks to God for their success. And that success continued when they became the 'shock' team of the competition after they reached the quarter finals after beating Greece on penalties, However, their superb run then ended when they lost on penalties to Holland.

2014 World Cup: Nigeria's on-field prayer huddle

The Nigerian team showed the importance to them of their religious beliefs in their practice on the field of forming a circle in the centre of the pitch with their goalkeeper Enyeama leading the team in prayers. They did this before the start, before the second half, and also after the game ended in all their four World Cup matches.

2014 World Cup: BBC produce a special short film on God

The importance of religion in the World Cup was well illustrated by Dan Walker's piece shown on BBC TV on July 4th before the semi-finals started. In it there were visual clips of players in the earlier stages of this World Cup praying with their words shown on the screen. It seemed clear that the creation of such a short film on the importance of religion in this competition was almost certainly thought of as the tournament progressed rather than before it started. That very short film could so easily have been called 'The God Squad in the Brazil World Cup.'

Now for TWO players, one a veteran, the other a youngster who are clearly members of the God Squad.

The World famous Brazilian — Philippians 4:13

You may never have heard of the footballer Ricardo Izecson dos Santos Leite yet as a sports fan you will certainly have seen him play with Kaka on the back of his shirt. He is now in the autumn of his career having left AC Milan in the summer of 2014 before playing in America in the MLS. His CV includes being FIFA's World Footballer of The Year, winner of the European Ballon d'Or, and he has World Cup and Champions League winners' medals, plus countless other honours.

Yet all his soccer skills, all his honours and all his medals he says were 'gifts from God', and famously after AC Milan won the Champions League in 2007 he took off his club shirt to reveal his T-shirt that stated that 'I belong to Jesus.' After he helped Brazil win the 2002 World Cup with an attitude of gratitude he prayed on the pitch as, 'I thank God for all my victories.' He also reportedly gives one tenth of his income to the Church.

His favourite book is the Bible, and if Isaiah 54:17 was Ray Lewis' favourite then for Kaka it was Philippians 4:13 which states that 'in him who strengthens me I am able for anything'.

But does his faith actually matter in football terms? The answer has to be an emphatic 'Yes' as his greatest qualities on the field are his calmness, composure, and control and those three are to a large extent an expression of his faith, and they give him the concentrated focus that enables the considerable football skills of this attacking midfielder to flow.

2014 West Bromwich Albion striker Saido Berahino. 'God has been a big influence in my life and my faith helped me through.'

Berahino was just ten years old when he came to England from war-torn Burundi and he soon made a big impact at West Brom's academy. He graduated to the first team before in the 2013/14 season his career went off course when he was photographed taking laughing gas and also when he was punched by a team mate in a dressing room bust-up when the club was fighting relegation. It was a very difficult time for the young striker. However, The Baggies avoided relegation, and in the new 2014/15 season with new manager Alan Irvine's support and encouragement Berahino thrived scoring 8 goals in his first 11 Premier League games. As a result the under 21 international earned a call up to the England squad amid stories that top clubs wanted to sign him for £20 million.

However, he was in no doubt that his Christian beliefs had seen him through the tough times and enabled him to become so successful. 'God has been a big influence in my life and my faith helped me through'.

GOLF: THE PLAYERS DEVOTIONAL

'We invite you to join us in spreading the Word of Christ and in glorifying God'

In America the Players Devotional is compiled by the US Professional Golf Association. So a number of Tour players, their wives, caddies and mentors read, pray and discuss a particular Biblical text in the morning of each tournament day before their tee times. It started in 2009 when pro golfer Ben Crane and his caddy Joel Stock realised that their first priority each day was to glorify and honour God.

For example in the week of the 2014 AT+T Pebble Beach National Pro-Am that was played over the four days from Thursday Feb 6th to Sunday Feb 9th the four Biblical texts to be studied were Matthew 5:3 on Thursday, followed by 5:4 on Friday, 5:5 on Saturday and 5:6 on Sunday.

There is a very long list of USPGA Tour players, often with their wives, who are part of the Devotional — they include major winners Bubba Watson, Zach Johnson, Webb Simpson, Stewart Cink, Tom Lehman and

Davis Love, as well as tour winners like Scott Stallings and Aaron Baddeley who incidentally would have become a preacher if he hadn't been a pro golfer. From the very many examples of US golfers who attribute their success to their faith I have chosen just three JB Holmes, Webb Simpson and Zach Johnson.

May 2014: JB Holmes — 'I want to thank my Lord and Saviour for being with me all week.'

Since the second of his two USPGA tour wins in 2008 loss of form and two operations including brain surgery had combined to stop JB from winning again.

So immediately after his comeback victory in May 2014 after his final winning putt had dropped, when interviewed live on TV Holmes' first words were, 'I want to thank my Lord and Saviour for being with me all week.' He clearly felt that after six winless years and two long lay-offs that his return to winning ways had been based on his Christian beliefs.

In horse racing parlance if this had been a racing victory, in breeding terms it would surely have been — JB Wins Again by God Squad out of the Comeback Trail, and we'll return to the massive motivating power of the Comeback Trail in Chapter 9.

2012: Webb Simpson — 'I felt the Lord telling me just to be patient.'

Webb Simpson joined the USPGA Tour in 2009 and in his third year in 2011 he was in contention 9 times winning twice as well as losing in a play-off, before the following year in June 2012 he won one of golf's four major tournaments, The US Open. In less than 12 months he'd gone from 'Webb Who?' to a three-time winner including a Major championship. There was no doubt in Webb's mind that his success was based on his religious faith. After his breakthrough win in the Wyndhams Championship in August 2011 he said 'I'd be stupid not to thank my Lord and Saviour Jesus Christ...I felt his presence all day,' and again after his US Open win, 'I had a peace all day. I probably prayed more the last 3 holes than I ever did in my life.'

In golf mental composure is crucial to success in any tournament especially in a Major tournament like the US Open, and Simpson's success has been built on that mentality, 'I felt the Lord telling me just to be patient.'

I keep a record of all golfers who are in contention on the final day of every golf tournament and Webb Simpson's record from August 2011 up to and including his US Open win was excellent. He'd bettered the average score of the leading contenders by 2 or more shots 6 times in those 8 events in which he was in contention.

That is the record of a player who remains calm under the severest of final round pressure and that calmness he said came from his faith.

However, the Nappy Factor was also at work in Webb's progress as he became a first-time dad, of a son, in February 2011. He went on to win his first tournament six months later, when his wife and baby James were at the green side to greet his maiden victory. The following year in 2012, in his first full Nappy Factor year, Webb won the US Open when his wife was pregnant carrying their second child, daughter Willow, who was born just six weeks after that Major victory.

So Webb's composed, calm and relaxed approach probably had two sources — his deeply held religious faith and the positive Nappy Factor effect caused by the birth of his first child, a son, and by his wife's second pregnancy.

2007: Zach Johnson — Psalm 16:8 — the 2007 US Masters 'My Lord was walking with me.'

Zach is a Church speaker who has a deep Christian faith, and on the day before he won the 2007 US Masters a local minister sent Zach a text message — it was Psalm 16:8 'I have set the Lord always before me. Because he is at my right hand, I will not be shaken.'

The next day, Easter Sunday, Zach wasn't shaken as he went on to win the 2007 US Masters after posting a superb final round 69 to win by two strokes with Tiger Woods one of three players tied second. After his triumph his comments were predictable as he said, 'This being Easter, I cannot help but believe my Lord and Saviour was walking with me. I owe this to him,' and he immediately shook hands with his good friend and devout Christian Aaron Baddeley who as a 200/1 outsider had won the Verizon Heritage tournament on Easter Sunday 12 months earlier. As you'd expect the fact that two devout Christian friends had won on successive Easter Sundays was not seen as a coincidence rather as an example of divine intervention.

Bernhard Langer — The born again Christian

So far we have looked at three American golfers who are definitely members of the God Squad. So let's now look at a star European golfer, the German Bernhard Langer who we first came across in Chapter 3 on Landmark birthdays. Brought up as a regular Roman Catholic churchgoer he had been an altar boy for several years so he was already a Christian as he successfully made his way in the golfing world. Indeed he had won 11 times on the European Tour before the 27-year-old won the US Masters at Augusta in 1985.

A week after that first Major win he went to a Bible study class with his wife Vicki and there they became 'born again Christians'. Bernhard admitted that before his 'conversion' his priorities had been golf, golf, and yet more golf. Since then Bernhard has had what he called 'a personal relationship with Christ' and that has enabled him to increase his on course composure, calmness and focus and also to put golf into perspective enabling him to cope with any issues relating to either his golfing or his more personal non-golfing life.

After he was 'born again' he won in every one of the next 11 years with 22 wins in that time including another US Masters triumph in 1993.

However, what happened in 1991 was to create the 'Langer Legend' so we'll return to him for the third time in the chapter on 'Mental Let Down'.

An assessment of The God Squad — can and does religious faith improve sporting performance?

In case all the Biblical quotes, and religious examples suggest I have a bias in favour of religious faith let me stress at once that I am an atheist and a member of the British Humanist Association so I most definitely do not believe in a God or in any after life.

Nevertheless it is clear to me that a sportsman who holds and genuinely practices a religious faith can derive crucial benefits from it, even if, of course, those positive effects do not in themselves in any way give any credibility at all to the subject of his faith. However, the validity of any religious faith is not our concern here because In this book we simply want to discover, exemplify and assess the more unusual factors that can and do affect sporting performance and if we ask can religious faith have a positive impact on sporting performance the answer is clearly yes it most definitely can, and yes it most definitely does.

Religious Faith can work positively in a sporting context in three ways.

First, before a sporting event, by providing the believer with a wider sense of perspective so enabling him to realise that sport is only sport, and although important it is simply a part of life. This sense of perspective can be crucial as it enables the sportsman to relax when playing. We saw this in the Bernhard Langer example how becoming a born again Christian enabled him to change his priorities so that he put golf into perspective which enabled him to have a continual run of success.

Second, as we saw with the Baltimore Ravens, religious faith can be used to create a driving motivation such that the players believed winning was inevitable, indeed they felt it was their destiny to win the 2013 Super Bowl.

Third, during a sporting event, especially when the pressure is at its height, when receiving the football for a vital touchdown in American football, when facing a crucial 10 foot putt, or when having the chance to score a decisive goal in a big football match, faith can enable a sportsman to possess that vitally important feeling of calmness, composure, and control so essential for success.

Nevertheless is there a conflict between religious faith and being a tough competitor?

The answer as we have seen has to be an emphatic 'No'. On the contrary faith can enable individuals and teams to become really hard to beat. The simplistic notion that those who are in 'The God Squad' are somehow soft 'pushovers' is simply untrue!

However, it is possible for team spirit to be badly affected by religious faith.

There is the possibility that in a team sport the deep-seated religious beliefs of a few team members could have an unsettling effect on one or two of their colleagues. In his book 'Red Card Roy' footballer Roy McDonough wrote about how Cambridge United struggled in the 1984/85 season, and he was scathing in his criticism of three of his team mates Alan Comfort, Graham Daniels, and David Moyes stating that the three of them would sit in the changing room with a little black book, presumably The Bible, discussing their beliefs when McDonough felt that they should have been 'psyching themselves up' for a relegation scrap. He thought they were too nice on the pitch wondering why, referring to David Moyes, a big ginger jock from Glasgow Celtic who bleated about Jesus could play with so little aggression.

It is difficult to evaluate this 'evidence' as it may have been over emphasised to boost sales yet we do know that Graham Daniels went on to become General Director of Christians in Sport, Alan Comfort became a vicar, while David Moyes went on to build a reputation as a top class manager at Everton before his disastrous eleven months spell as Sir Alex Ferguson's successor at Manchester United which was followed in November 2014 by his appointment as manager of the Spanish club Real Sociedad. Nevertheless the fact that one player was so annoyed by his three Christian team mates shows that religious belief has in the past led to team disunity.

However, let's remember that McDonough's criticism was 30 years ago and we should note that it was based on a rather dated view of how football should be played. The days of 'bite yer legs' players who 'got stuck in' have tended to give way to faster, fitter players whose key defensive skills are the ability to concentrate on closing down players, running into space, to 'press' the man in possession, to read the game and to win the ball by intercepting passes rather than by the traditional crunching tackle.

In today's football players of different religions play alongside each other in the Premier League with their sole concern being their team mates' willingness to work, run and shoot rather than their religious views.

FINALLY

I hope you don't think The God Squad is a derogatory term as actually it's a rhyming, and therefore more memorable, term than say The God Factor, or The Religious Factor.

Although 'The Faith Factor' could have been used it is a weaker phrase and there are many sportsmen who have a faith but it is not a really important or a deeply influential part of their lives — remember the second group of believers who we identified at the start of this chapter?

I also prefer The God Squad as it has a sense of a collective of people whose faiths can have positive effects on their sporting careers.

Discover more Sports Analysis Secrets at elliottsportanalysis.co.uk

CHAPTER SIX
THE GAY FACTOR

In this book we are examining factors that can affect sporting performance so I wondered if one factor could be the 'coming out' in public of a gay sportsman or woman as it seems clear that telling the world you are gay has a positive, relaxing and liberating effect. So let's have a look first at how many have 'come out', and especially when they have made their announcement. Then we can analyse the evidence so far, and assess how significant this factor is now and how important it may become in the future.

Please note that there are sportsmen who are 'known' to be gay but have chosen NOT to 'come out' and that decision commands respect so they are excluded from the analysis in this chapter.

Gay athletes if they choose to 'come out' must decide when to do so. This very important timing decision can fall into any one of THREE categories.

1. After their career has ended.
2. Towards the end of their career.
3. During their playing career.

Of all the sportsmen and women who have 'come out' the vast majority did so AFTER their career had ended. Here are TWELVE examples taken from SEVEN different sports.

BASEBALL
In 1982, two years after he retired, Glen Burke became the first former American pro baseball star to state that he was gay. He had been drafted by the LA Dodgers in 1976 and he retired early in 1980 because as he said 'prejudice drove me out.' He died of aids in 1995 aged 42.

AMERICAN FOOTBALL
There were two notable NFL American footballers who 'came out' before 2000.

*   Dave Kopay, after playing in the NFL for five teams from 1964-72 announced he was gay in 1975, followed two years later by the publication of his book, 'The Dave Kopay Story'.

*   Roy Simmons after playing for the New York Giants and the Washington Redskins announced he was gay in 1992.

This millennium there have been three more American footballers who came out after their playing careers had ended.

- Esera Tuaolo's nine season career as a nose tackle ended in 2000, and he 'came out' two years later.
- More recently Wade Davis, the former Tennessee Titan, finished his career in 2003, yet he didn't announce he was gay until 2012.
- Kwame Harris was the 26th draft pick back in 2003 and after playing for the San Francisco 49ers and the Oakland Raiders he retired in 2010, he 'came out' three years later.

BASKETBALL
John Amaechi was a star basketball player who retired in 2003. He 'came out' in February 2007 on ESPN TV, and later his book 'Man in the middle' that told his life story was published and he has gone on to be a renowned public speaker.

DIVING
Greg Louganis was an American diving champion who had a glittering career in which he won 47 National titles, 13 World Championships, was the first diver to be given a 'perfect 10' score, and he won two gold medals in each of the Olympics in 1984 and 1988 so he really was a huge star. He retired in 1989 and first admitted he was gay in 1995 before a year later in his autobiography *Breaking the Surface* he told his life story. The book became a best seller and was made into a film.

GYMNASTICS
Aussie gymnast Ji Wallace won a silver medal in the 2000 Olympics in Sydney. After his retirement he announced he was gay in 2003.

FOOTBALL
Olivier Rouyer was a French footballer with 17 international caps who came out after both his playing and coaching career had ended in 1994.
Thomas Hitzlsperger retired from football after persistent injuries in 2013, he had won 52 international caps for Germany, and the ex-midfielder had played in the Premier League for West Ham, Everton and mainly at Aston Villa. He announced he was gay in January 2014.

SWIMMING
In July 2014 two years after he retired 31-year-old Aussie star swimmer Ian Thorpe said he was gay in an interview with Michael Parkinson. Thorpe, nicknamed the Torpedo, had been a swimming superstar breaking 22 world records and winning 5 Olympic Gold medals. Later that month he joined the BBC broadcasting team covering the Commonwealth Games in Glasgow.

Several sportsmen and women have 'come out' TOWARDS THE END of

their careers. Here are SEVEN examples from FIVE different sports — Basketball, Hurling, Rugby Union, Football, and Women's football.

- **Justin Fashanu** was the first black player to be transferred for £1million when in 1981 he moved to Nottingham Forest who were managed by Brian Clough. Sadly his relationship with his manager broke down allegedly because Clough believed that Justin was gay. Indeed in his autobiography Clough recalled how he asked Justin why, when he went out at night, he went to 'a bloody poof's club?' And the use of that language tells its own story! After leaving Forest Fashanu's career spiralled downwards as he went to a succession of British clubs before playing in America and Canada. He came out in October 1990, and after many troubled years he was found hanged in May 1998.

- **Jason Collins** is an American professional basketball player who on leaving Stanford University in the 2001 draft was the 18th overall pick so this guy was one of the big Basketball stars of his year with his defensive skills his key attribute. However, he didn't 'come out' until 12 years later after the 2012/2013 season, and in February 2014 he became the first publicly gay Basketball player when he joined, the seventh team of his career, the Brooklyn Nets on a 10 day contract and on his debut he helped The Nets to a 96-80 win over the Chicago Bulls.

- **Donal Og Cusack** and his brother **Conor Cusack** were star Irish hurling players who played for Cork. Donal Og became the first openly gay Irish sportsman when he 'came out' in October 2009 four years before he retired. His brother Conor announced he was gay four years later in 2013.

- **Casey Stoney** is a defender who plays for Arsenal women's team. She had 116 caps for England when at 31 years of age, inspired by diver Tom Daley's recent 'coming out', she announced she was gay in February 2014.

- **Gareth Thomas** made 100 appearances for his country and went on three overseas Tours with the British Lions so he was a top class Rugby Union player. He came out in 2009 14 years after winning his first cap, and a year later he moved to play Rugby League retiring in October 2011.

- **Robbie Rogers** Finally there is the unusual case of footballer Robbie Rogers who made his name in America playing for Columbus Crew before he joined Championship side Leeds United. However, his time with the Yorkshire club was blighted by injury and after he left Leeds in February 2013 he announced he was gay. However, Robbie, who had played 18 times for the USA international side, returned to America where he joined LA Galaxy in May 2013 so becoming the first openly gay footballer to play in the MLS, the American soccer league. So here we have a unique case of a player who had planned to 'come out' after he retired and then decided to play on although clearly his best footballing days were a very long way behind him.

SIX sportsmen in FOUR different sports have announced they were gay DURING THEIR PLAYING CAREER in the last ten years.

The first three examples all come from the same sport — 10-metre platform diving.

• **Matt Mitcham** Australian diver Matt Mitcham as a teenager had fought depression and then retired for nine months from diving before he made a comeback. Just a few months before competing in the 2008 Olympics when giving a press interview in Sydney he was asked who he lived with and inadvertently he said he had lived for two years with his partner. 'I hadn't planned to do it at all' so this 'coming out' had clearly been unplanned, unintended yet unforgettable. A few months later he and his partner both went to the Beijing Olympics as Matt was in the 3-metre springboard, in which he finished 16th, and also in his main event the 10-metre platform dive. That 10-metre platform final was truly amazing as with one dive left Matt was well behind star Chinese diver Zhou Luxin. However, Luxin's final dive was extremely poor so Matt had a chance although he still had to produce under the maximum possible pressure an extremely good final dive, and that's just what the Aussie did. His final dive was absolutely outstanding earning him 4 'perfect ten' scores and a total score that was one of the highest for a single 10-metre platform dive in Olympic History. Matt had won and so the first Aussie to win a diving gold since 1924 was an openly gay man winning with his partner in the audience!

• **Mathew Helm** However, Matt wasn't the first openly gay Australian man to win an Olympic diving medal as Mathew Helm had done so four years earlier in the Athens Olympics when he won a silver medal in the 10-metre platform event. Earlier he had won silver in the World Championships in Barcelona, and later in the 2006 Commonwealth Games in Melbourne.

• **Tom Daley** Another 10-metre platform diver is British teenager Tom Daley who at 19 'came out' in early December 2013. Tom won a bronze medal in a blaze of publicity in the 2012 London Olympics. In preparation for his attempt to win gold in the 2016 Rio de Janiero Olympics, in the same week that he announced that he was gay he also changed his coach as he replaced Andy Banks with 50-year-old Jane Figueiredo who had a top-class CV, a great reputation as a diving trainer in American collegiate sport and an impressive Olympic record. His former coach Andy Banks, who had coached him from his early years, accepted Tom's reasoning and it is said that they would keep in touch so the 'parting' appeared amicable. So here we have a very young and successful sportsman with his career ahead of him coming out as gay when still a teenager.

The other examples cover THREE different sports — Cricket, Boxing, and American Football.

CRICKET

Steve Davies When Steve Davies 'came out' publicly in late February 2011 he became the first cricketer to do so. He plays for Surrey and is a wicket-keeper/batsman who opens the batting in first class and limited over cricket. He had been selected by England for the 2010/11 Ashes tour and as that three month tour approached he felt it was the right time to let his team mates know that he was gay, and it was after that tour in February 2011 that Steven went public.

He had been selected for that Tour as the understudy to wicket-keeper/ batsman Matt Prior who kept his form so well that Steve didn't play for England who won that Ashes series 3-1.

BOXING

Orlando Cruz When featherweight boxer Orlando Cruz announced he was gay on October 4th 2012 he became the only active boxer to do so. Although boxing is the most macho of all individual sports his promoter and his friends stayed loyal to him. In his first fight after his announcement he beat Jorge Pazos on a unanimous points decision, and then went on to stop Aalan Martinez in the 6th round in March 2013. Later that year he challenged Orlando Salido for the NBO World Featherweight title with Salido the long odds on hot favourite. Cruz was outclassed taking some really punishing shots to both head and body before the fight was stopped in the 7th round.

AMERICAN FOOTBALL

Michael Sam In February 2014 we had a unique example of a young athlete very early in his career and in an ultra-macho, violent team sport 'coming out' when Michael Sam said, 'I'm an American footballer and I'm gay.' Sam is a 24-year-old, 6 foot 2 inches, 18 stone defensive end and in his last season as a college player for the University of Missouri Tigers he was named as the defensive player of the year in the South Eastern Conference.

The annual draft in American football enables the NFL clubs to recruit the best of that year's college players so in the 2014 draft on May 10th

Michael Sam became the first openly gay player to be involved in that draft process. He was the 249th pick when St Louis Rams selected him and then live on TV, crying with emotion, he kissed his partner. That kiss and the fact that St Louis is in Missouri and under current Missouri law an individual can be refused employment on the grounds of their sexuality has inevitably sparked a vigorous debate.

There will therefore inevitably be massive media interest in Sam's future, and we will return to him in our end of chapter assessment.

ASSESSMENT

Compared to staying silent 'coming out' has three massive potential advantages for any gay sportsman or woman.

'I'm not fighting two opponents any longer and that is a great relief'

First there is a huge sense of relief as shown in the above quote from boxer Orlando Cruz who also said that, 'The nights of staying awake and crying are over,' while footballer Robbie Rogers stated that, 'Life is simple when the secret has gone. Gone is the pain at work, the pain from avoiding questions, and at last the pain from hiding such a deep secret.'

'To make the most of his ability a sportsman needs to focus on his sport and that is so much easier if his personal life is happy and stable'

This was a quote from Rugby Union star Gareth Thomas, who came out in 2009, which illustrates the point that once a sporting star has 'come out' he or she can walk down the street, go to a concert or have a drink at a bar with his or her partner without the worry of someone popping up with a mobile phone to take the picture that could be on the internet and in the papers within 24 hours.

'I had hundreds and hundreds of letters saying how much I'd helped them...The support I got was overwhelming...the response has been amazing...I honestly had no problems'

When cricketer Steve Davies 'came out' in 2011 he was the first cricketer to do so, and as the above quotes show he was amazed at the positive reaction he'd received. Steve said after Tom Daley's announcement that he was gay in December 2013, that 'when the dust settles there will be thousands of people contacting Tom to thank him for what he has done... not just young kids but older guys and girls too'.

It must surely increase a sport star's personal sense of self-worth to know that their decision to state publicly that they are gay can have such a widespread positive impact on so many people.

THE POTENTIAL RISKS OF 'COMING OUT'

Does 'coming out' affect sponsorship deals and media work?

Negative impact

You'll recall that Aussie diver Matt Mitcham won the 10-metre platform diving gold medal in 2008 in the Beijing Olympics. However, after that success there were no corporate sponsorship offers in 2009 although in 2010 he got financial support from Telstra, an Aussie telecommunications company before in 2011 he became the sporting ambassador for the interestingly named, Funky Trunks. Matt himself was convinced that his sexuality had been a major impediment to attracting corporate sponsors

Positive impact

Nigel Currie, a director at the leading sports agency brand Rapport, when speaking about Tom Daley's sponsorship prospects after the diver 'came out' in December 2013 said that he thought it may actually improve Tom's marketability because of what he had done and the way he had handled it. He went on to suggest that in the modern world sponsors and brands in general had become much more flexible and broad in their views. Indeed with companies very conscious of their image and their social responsibility he went on to say that they want to appeal to as broad a spectrum as possible and they were not going to let past barriers get in the way. These comments were borne out as Tom Daley's media career, which started with his appearances in Splash in January 2014, developed further in April when 'Tom Daley goes global' was shown on ITV2 in a programme that featured Tom on a backpacking adventure starting in Thailand.

Also on the positive side there is an interesting conversation reported in the 2014 biography of retired former England footballer, centre back, Sol Campbell. After telling the sportswear producer Puma that he was not gay he was told that they had actually hoped that he was as they were keen to represent the first international gay footballer as they could sell many more boots as it would be a worldwide story! So, as Martin Samuel pointed out in the Daily Mail, there is a school of thought that thinks that if, say, an individual Premier League footballer 'came out' he would be fully sponsored and marketed globally as he would become a gay icon although this would probably not happen if several footballers all announced they were gay at the same time.

DIFFICULTY OF FINDING WORK WITHIN YOUR OWN SPORT AFTER RETIREMENT

For those who come out after retirement getting sports related jobs may become difficult. Dave Kopay the American footballer who 'came out' in 1975 believed that he couldn't get coaching work after he 'came out'. However, almost 40 years ago in the mid-seventies seems 'light years' away from the changing attitudes, especially among the younger generations of today.

The problem getting a job working as a coach or as a writer or analyst will probably now only apply to players who announce they are gay very late in their careers or after they have retired. If an increasing number of younger sportsmen and women 'come out' early in their careers this potential problem is unlikely to occur many years later when they retire.

MEDIA ATTENTION

Inevitably in the short term after the 'coming out' announcement the sportsman will have to face the print and visual media with the coverage they receive being dependent on their fame and the importance of their sport.

In the case of American footballer Michael Sam who 'came out' early in 2014 when just 24 years old it was always certain that he would attract a 'media-circus' from the very start.

THE POTENTIAL DISTRACTION

Once a sports star has 'come out' during his career he or she will most probably, as we saw earlier with the example of cricketer Steve Davies, be surprised by the letters they receive and the support they get. This new and unexpected support could then act as a distraction as attention is paid to responding to letters and possibly working for gay rights so preventing the necessary 100% focus needed for sporting success. So although it would be highly laudable if a sports star was to use his or her status to become to some degree a campaigner it is likely that such activity could adversely effect the star's sporting focus especially in the short term.

THE DIFFERENCE BETWEEN INDIVIDUAL AND TEAM SPORTS

It is probably much easier to 'come out' early in your career in an individual sport than in a team sport. In an individual sport if your coach and immediate technical staff are supportive then although 'coming out' remains difficult and requires real courage, it is probably easier than it would be for a team player for two key reasons.

In a team sport you still have to have the support of the coach and technical staff yet unlike the guy in the individual sport you also have a number of team-mates whose response to an openly gay team mate could range from unwelcoming to the downright hostile within the macho environment of the dressing room.

Secondly, there are few individual sports which have the massive crowds of 30,000 to 80,000 that can watch the macho team sports like Football, American football, Rugby Union, or Rugby League. As Casey Stoney, the England international footballer, said after she 'came out' in February 2014, 'I empathise with male soccer players who don't want to come out ... there's so much media pressure, who'd want to be that person? The male terraces are brutal ... there's not 50,000 at our games.' Although what Casey said about the male terraces was true she hadn't foreseen that the first women's match at Wembley would attract 45,619 which was the crowd for the international match between England and Germany on Sunday November 23rd 2014.

In the meantime the key question is — does 'coming out' lead to improved sporting performance?

The evidence we have comes from the six sportsmen who have 'come out' as openly gay during their careers. However, statistically speaking that is a very small sample number so we cannot draw many definite conclusions.

Two Aussie 10-metre divers succeed when openly gay

We do know for certain that success at the highest sporting level is attainable after 'coming out' as we have two outstanding examples albeit from the same sport of 10-metre platform diving. Matt Mitcham with his sensational dive that won Olympic gold in Beijing in 2008 and earlier from another Aussie Mathew Helm who had won silver in the 2004 Athens Olympics.

Tom Daley On his own admission since his bronze medal in London 2012 Tom Daley has suffered from Post Olympic Letdown. His 'coming out' was immediately followed by a change of coach and there has been speculation that being a TV star he has embraced a celebrity lifestyle because he'd lost his appetite for his sport, but not for chocolate! One thing is certain his form undoubtedly worsened in the early months of 2014. His key dive is his back two and a half somersault with a two and a half twist, and in April he admitted that he was fearful when doing it as the thrill and expectation of success had been replaced by a 'fear factor' so he has sought psychological help. Tom had a disappointing start to the year exemplified by his failure to win a medal in the World Series in April. Nevertheless on August 2nd in the Commonwealth Games in the 10-metre platform event he comfortably won the gold medal. However, the opposition was not strong with the 2008 Olympic champion Matt Mitcham a poor fourth.

Tom now knows that he must improve significantly if he is to win a medal in Rio against very strong Chinese opposition. However, in his own sport he is aware that openly gay divers Matt Mitcham and Mathew Helm won Olympic gold and silver so he understands that 'coming out' is no barrier at all to success in his sport. Overall we can say that Tom is still a very young man who has had a lot of changes in a very short time in both his sporting and personal life. The challenge he now faces is to fully regain the focus, determination, and hunger he had leading up to the 2012 London Olympics.

Michael Sam Sam's role as a defensive end is to 'rush the passer' however, the Rams already had Robert Quinn, Chris Long, and William Hayes. So it wasn't a surprise when Sam who is regarded as a good but not outstanding player didn't make either the Rams' roster or their practice squad.

He then moved to join the practice squad of the Dallas Cowboys. However, he didn't make their 53 man roster and they also released him.

Having read several articles about Michael Sam it appears that his size and physique — he's 6 foot 2 inches and 261 pounds, plus his one-dimensional style of play rather than the fact that he is gay are the reasons that so far he's been unable to make any NFL roster.

Steve Davies
Davies' cricketing career seemed to plateau as it continued at a similar standard to that before he 'came out'.

Orlando Cruz
Cruz did win his two subsequent Featherweight fights although he lost when challenging for the NBO World title. However, it seems clear that in that fight he was simply outclassed and would have lost against Salido irrespective of his announcement that he was gay.

Apart from Michael Sam in American football, we have no recent example of any player during their career 'coming out' in the macho male team sports of Football, Rugby Union, Rugby League, and American football. Nevertheless in individual sports such as Boxing and Cricket the evidence is neutral while in diving it is undoubtedly positive.

FINALLY — 'THE TIMES THEY ARE A CHANGING'
In the 'good old days' when 'big men didn't cry', when a depressed man had to 'pull himself together', when real men sweated in manufacturing industry to bring home the pay packet for 'her indoors', homophobia ruled OK?

However, the changing role of women, the move from manufacturing towards services, and the growth of technology have led to a massive change in the roles of men and women which coupled with a growth of liberal thinking has smashed down many of the walls of discrimination that definitely used to exist. Whoever thought that we would now have 'house husbands' or black quarterbacks in American football?

Slowly but surely homophobia, although sadly still alive and thriving in several countries, is diminishing as the new younger generations' attitudes are generally so different from that of many of their parents. There is a growing steady disgust of homophobia. However, although there have been seven prominent 'coming out' announcements by sportsmen and women from January 2013 to July 2014 there are still no openly gay footballers or golfers, no gay Formula 1 drivers, and male lawn tennis is also a gay-free zone.

Nevertheless if present trends continue I can see a time within a generation when 'coming out' will be a thing of the past as it will become accepted that a person's sexuality simply does not need a public announcement.

CHAPTER SEVEN
INSPIRATION BY COMPARISON

'Comparisons are odious'

So often when we make comparisons we compare with someone else who has a higher salary, bigger house, or better lifestyle. We tend to compare with those who in one way or another seem to have 'more' or 'better' than us. Such comparisons so easily lead to feelings of envy, jealousy, and the unfairness of the world. So often when driving down the road of comparisons we are driving down a one way street and it's invariably a bumpy journey that ends in frustration, disappointment and often anger.

On the other hand in sport some comparisons can be highly motivational so let's get aboard 'The Comparison Train' and see where it takes us.

At any point in time in sport, whether in team or individual sports, there are two possible situations.

1. When there is no standard of comparison because the objective is 'impossible'

There are the potential achievements that seem impossible as no team or individual has ever previously achieved them before.

THE 4-MINUTE MILE

For a long time it was simply believed that it was probably impossible for the human body to run a sub 4-minute mile.

Anyone attempting to do so didn't know that it was possible they just hoped it might be. They couldn't be inspired by other athletes' achievements because nobody had ever run a sub 4-minute mile. There was simply no standard of comparison.

The world mile record held by the Swede Gundar Haegg stood at 4 minutes 1.4 seconds until on the 6th May 1954 at the Iffley track in Oxford, after skilled pace setting by Chris Brasher and Chris Chataway, Roger Bannister took the lead and when he breasted the tape utterly exhausted he had clocked 3 minutes 59.4 seconds so the elusive sub 4-minute mile had been achieved.

EVEREST

A similar 'impossible' feat had been achieved just under 12 months earlier when New Zealander Edmund Hillary and the Nepalese Sherpa Tenzing Norgay reached the 29,035 foot summit of Mount Everest, the world's highest mountain. Set in the Himalayas along the border of Nepal, and Tibet the freezing weather, the potential for falls, the deep crevasses and the 'mountain sickness' caused by the high altitude plus the need to carry all food and supplies had, like the 4-minute mile, led to the widely held belief that to reach the summit was impossible. However, the British Everest Expedition led by Colonel John Hunt succeeded at 11.30am on May 29th 1953 when Hillary and Tenzing were 'on top of the world'. Interesting that after that triumph one paper in jest wondered whatever next — a man on the moon!

2. 'Inspiration By Comparison' [IBC]
Inspiration By Comparison occurs when a sportsman sees someone else's success and thinks that if he can do it so can I.

There can be no doubt at all that Roger Bannister's achievement in May 1954 inspired every other mile running athlete, and that after Sir Edmund Hillary and Sherpa Tenzing had reached the peak of Everest virtually every other climber and, as we shall see, one female non-climber believed they could do so too.

'I predicted that once I had broken the four-minute mile everybody would find it much easier'.

In the words of the man himself, 'It was a long time coming...there was a psychological barrier with it. I predicted that once I had broken the four-minute mile everybody would find it much easier. Apres moi, le deluge. And there was.'

Other athletes then knew it was possible and six weeks later on June 21st the Aussie John Landy reduced Bannister's World Record by almost two full seconds bringing it down to 3 minutes 58 seconds.

Over the following years breaking the four-minute mile seemed almost commonplace. Indeed on May 28th 1955 just over a year after the first sub four-minute mile a time of under four minutes wasn't enough to win or even come second in the mile at the British Games in London as third-placed Brian Hewson discovered.

Over the subsequent years the world record for the mile was regularly lowered with it falling below 3 minutes 50 seconds in 1975 when New Zealander John Walker ran 3.49.4 in Sweden, and it had fallen to 3 minutes 43.13 by the end of the millennium, an astonishing 16.27 seconds faster than that achieved on that historic day in Oxford 45 years earlier.

THE EVEREST EFFECT
Since the summit of Everest was reached we have seen the same impact as we saw with the four-minute mile with countless mountaineers inspired to 'have a go' at the world's highest mountain.

We have had young and old, male and female climbers reaching the summit with the youngest the Nepalese Temba Tsheri who reached the top in 2001 when 16. In 1998 at the age of 23 Bear Grylls became the youngest

British climber to reach the summit only to be displaced in 2001 by Rob Gauntlett who conquered Everest as a 19-year-old — sadly he died two years later when climbing the Alps. In May 2010 22-year-old Bonita Norris became the youngest ever British woman to successfully reach the peak and that came just two years after she made the extraordinary decision to tackle Everest — a decision that astonished her family as she had never previously been a climber at all!

It is now over 60 years since that day when Sir Edmund Hillary and Sherpa Tenzing reached the summit and since then countless others have followed. However, the absurd notion that Everest is safe and easy was completely dispelled when early in 2014 sixteen Sherpas were tragically killed in a massive avalanche as a result of which Everest was effectively closed for the rest of the year.

From the vast number of IBC examples that I have amassed over the years I have chosen TWENTY THREE — with FIFTEEN of them drawn from 2014.

They are divided into FIVE different categories.

So let's look at these before seeing how IBC helped Ian Woosnam in two different ways to become the World's No 1 golfer, before my personal favourite alcoholic example!

IBC 1: Comparisons with those from your own country
2014: Australia
Greg Norman always maintained that of all the great sporting nations perhaps the Aussies are the best at inspiring each other — for example after Adam Scott had made his birdie putt on the 18th to win the 2013 US Masters he shouted 'C'mon Aussie', not 'C'mon Scotty'. Clearly he had thought of his country rather than himself in his moment of victory, Norman insisted that if they can't win, Aussies are desperate to see another Aussie win.

Adam Scott's win in the 2013 US Masters gave a huge boost to all Aussie golfers the impact of which fellow Aussie John Senden described as 'unbelievable'. So it proved in the early months of 2014 when first in mid-February Jason Day won the WGC/Matchplay in Arizona, and then just 4 weeks later John Senden won the Valspar Championship in Florida before two Aussies, Steven Bowditch [The Texas Open] and Matt Jones [The Shell Houston Open], both won for the first time in successive weeks in Texas tournaments. IBC had created a rolling March momentum as we had seen three Australians win in four weeks and at odds of 125/1, 300/1 and 125/1 they certainly weren't favourites but they certainly were inspired by the successes of their fellow countrymen!!

2013/14: France
'I think the French players are all very close' said Alexander Levy in April

2014 after he became the latest French player to win on the European tour, and this has been shown by their remarkable run of success with five European Tour wins in a 12 month period starting in late April 2013. In that time IBC clearly took effect with four winners in 2013 — Raphael Jacquelin in the Spanish Open, Gregory Bourdy in the Wales Open, Julien Quesne the Italian Open, and Victor Dubuisson the Turkish Airlines Open, before Alexander Levy's win in the 2014 China Open.

2010/11: South Africa

Louis Oosthuizen's win in the 2010 Open Golf Championship at St. Andrews was his first win in a major. His magnificent seven shot victory was a real inspiration to his very close friend and fellow countryman Charl Schwartzel who was just two years younger than Louis. In 2010 after Louis' win Charl went on to post his highest ever major finish when 18th in the USPGA before he too, like his friend Louis, won his first major when donning the famous green jacket after winning the 2011 US Masters at Augusta.

There was another classic earlier South African case of the IBC phenomena in 1997 involving their two star golfers Ernie Els, and Retief Goosen.

Ernie on the 15th June 1997 had won his second Major by winning the US Open for the second time, and the next week he won the Buick Classic. Just seven days later inspired by Ernie's back to back wins Retief Goosen looked a great bet at 33/1 to win the French Open as he seemed certain to be inspired by Els' performances and so it proved when the 'Goose' won by three shots and after his win he admitted that 'Watching Ernie play and seeing him do so well encouraged me to try to get up there as well.'

2007: Denmark

There are two unrelated Danish golfers Anders Hansen and Soren Hansen with Anders, born in September 1970 the elder by three and a half years. Anders posted his maiden win on 26th May 2002 winning the European Tour's 'flagship' tournament the Volvo PGA, and that win immediately inspired Soren who was 6th and 2nd in his next two events before on 30th May he too secured his first Tour win in the Murphy's Irish Open. After his win Soren explained that, 'when he [Anders] won, that was a boost for me as well.'

Remarkably in 2007 when Anders won for the second time it was again in the 'flagship' BMW PGA event. Soren, whose form had previously been very poor, suddenly improved with two 2nds and a 3rd before he too posted his second win when he won the Mercedes Benz Championship in September. As Soren said, 'Same old story. I don't want to lose ground to him so I've got to catch up.'

So they both secured their maiden European Tour wins within a month of each other, and their second victories in the same year.

IBC 2: Comparisons with those of a similar age
2014: Colin Montgomerie
We have already seen in Chapter 3 on Landmark birthdays the sensational form of the Spanish golfer Miguel Angel Jimenez once he had past 50 early in 2014. That spell of success had included his debut win on the Champions Tour in the Greater Gwinnett tournament in April in which Monty had finished 8th, and that win by Jimenez surely inspired Colin Montgomerie who in just his third start after Jimenez' success won the Seniors PGA — it was Monty's first ever win in America, and his first ever in a Major!! And, as we have seen, he went on to win another Major, the US Seniors' Open, in July.

2012/13: Darren Clarke
42-year-old Darren Clarke's win in the 2011 Open Championship at Royal St George's gave enormous pleasure to so many golf fans who had admired the courage, dignity and sheer class he had shown after the death of his wife in 2006 which we referred to in Chapter 4 on the Funeral Factor. With modern professional golf increasingly seen as a young man's game we can be sure that Darren's victory also gave real inspiration to the older pros. So no surprise when a year later another 42-year-old, Ernie Els, won The Open at Royal Lytham to be followed in 2013 by 44-year-old Phil Mickelson's first Open win when he lifted the famous claret jug at Muirfield. So we had three consecutive wins by players in their forties in the golf world's most prestigious golf major with IBC a contributory factor!

2010: Bonita Norris
Earlier in this chapter we noted 22-year-old Bonita Norris as she'd become the youngest British female to conquer Everest. After her triumph she said that she was inspired by male climber Bear Grylls, who had climbed Everest when he was only 23.

2001: Andrew Oldcorn
Another illustration of IBC by age came in 2001 when 41-year-old Andrew Oldcorn was the 150/1 'shock' winner of the Volvo PGA. After that success Andrew said that he'd read in the papers that 'Mark O'Meara was 41 when he won his first two majors. I was 41 this year and I still feel capable of winning here,' and win it he certainly did beating Angel Cabrera by two shots.

IBC 3: Comparisons with those in similar sporting or life positions
2014: Bournemouth manager Eddie Howe uses IBC to show that 'little clubs' can reach the Premier League.
In early November 2014 Bournemouth were top of the Championship which was an amazing achievement as just five years earlier amidst an appalling financial crisis they almost fell out of the Football League. So could football 'minnows' like Bournemouth really be expected to reach the Premier League? Manager Eddie Howe knew it was possible simply because it had been achieved by Burnley the previous season, and the

Lancashire club, like Bournemouth, was a small club with a small squad of players and a small budget. Howe said that they were 'looking at Burnley to see what can be achieved with a small squad and limited resources.... there are principles there that we can take' .Put simply if Burnley could reach the Premier League than so could Bournemouth. No doubt at all that this was IBC at work.

2014: Derby manager Steve McClaren uses IBC to motivate his players after their Wembley play-off defeat

The annual Championship play-off game at Wembley has the biggest prize to the winner of any individual football match on the planet as it brings the ever increasing financial rewards of being in the Barclays Premier League so to lose that match is always devastating. In the 2014 play-off match Derby County played really well yet lost the game in the last couple of minutes when the outplayed ten men of QPR got a breakaway goal. However, although deeply upset, Derby manager Steve McClaren took the IBC route to motivate his shattered players. The former England coach knew that in 2011 the beaten playoff finalists Reading went on in 2012 to gain promotion as champions, and so did Leicester City, who lost in the 2013 playoff final, and had just been runaway Champions in 2014. 'We'll look at the examples of Leicester and Reading. They had disappointment and went on to get promoted the next season.'

2014 Golfer G-Mac uses IBC with Slim Jim to re-invigorate his career

Graeme McDowell after playing with and against massively long drivers like Rory McIlroy, Dustin Johnson and Henrik Stenson had begun to ask himself whether he should bother to play as 'I was just a guy who hits it 275 yards and could only compete on short courses.' However, encouraged by European captain Paul McGinley telling him in advance of the Ryder Cup that he was to be first out in the singles because he was a fighter and a battler G-Mac began to re-focus on the skills and qualities he has rather than focus on the long driving that he hasn't got.

Crucially he needed a golfing role model and he found it in American Jim Furyk who like G-Mac is a short hitter yet a player who plays to his strengths which like G-Mac are his short game and his mental strength. After all Slim Jim ended the 2014 USPGA season with form figs of 4-2-15-5-8-23-4-2 winning almost $6 million, and Furyk at 44 is nine years older than McDowell. Clearly G-Mac's new end of year IBC thinking was that if short hitting Slim Jim can do it at 44 so could he at 35!!

2013: 'Coming out' as gay

We have already noted that 10-metre platform diver Tom Daley announced he was gay in December 2013 and as any sportsperson knows the history of his own chosen sport we can be sure that Tom knew of the two Aussie platform divers Mathew Helm and Matt Mitcham who had also 'come out' years earlier. He will surely have been inspired by the fact that as openly gay men they had both achieved Olympic success as Mathew Helm won silver in the 2004 Olympics, while Matt Mitcham in Beijing in 2008, under the greatest possible pressure produced that famous brilliant final dive to win the gold medal. So Tom knew for certain that it was possible to win Olympic gold and silver medals as an openly gay man because it had already been done.

2013/14: Choosing an early career path

In 2013 American golfers, Peter Uihlein and Brooks Koepka were both successful playing their golf on the European Tour and the Challenge Tour which is the feeder tour to the main tour.

The success of these two US players showed that playing in Europe made real sense for young ambitious American golfers so for the end of year 2013 Qualifying school there were a record number of US players entered with three of them earning their 2014 European Tour cards and one of them John Hahn saying that 'Peter and Brooks were a huge influence on me. I really never thought of coming over here because of the travel, but I saw what they did and the world ranking points that are available. I really have to thank them for showing me that it is worth coming here to play'. Again IBC was at work as young American golfers had started to think that if Uihlein and Koepka can do it so can I.

2014: Choosing a later career path

One of the key influences on 31-year-old Spurs striker Jermaine Defoe in his decision to sign for Toronto FC in January 2014 before the start of the American Major Soccer League [MLS] was the text he got from David Beckham who had played for the LA Galaxy in the MLS from 2007-2012. In it he told Jermaine that he'd love the MLS and be really impressed with Toronto's ambition. If a top English player like David Beckham could be so enthusiastic about and so successful in the MLS then Defoe felt he too could follow his example so he signed a 4-year contract. His new career got off to a flier in his first game when Toronto beat Seattle Sounders 2-1 thanks to two Defoe goals. Indeed Jermaine scored 11 goals in his first 16 matches before injury and loss of form soured relations and he became a free agent.

IBC 4: Comparisons with others who achieved 'shock' results
2014: Golf and first-time winners

The hardest thing for any sportsperson to achieve is that first breakthrough win. So in golf when one player achieves that maiden victory it inspires all the others still chasing that elusive first win and in early 2014 we saw an excellent example of this phenomenon when from March to the third week in May [excluding World Golf Championships and the US Masters], there were 6 first-time winners in the 10 tournaments on the USPGA tour. It was 'raining' first-timers as Chesson Hadley, Matt Every, Steven Bowditch, Matt Jones, Seung-Yul Noh, and Brendon Todd all entered the 'winners' enclosure for the first time.

2014: American Football

The 2014 Super Bowl was a triumph of youth over experience as Seattle Seahawks easily beat the favourites Denver Broncos by 43-8 in a very one sided game. The Seahawks had the second youngest team in Super Bowl history, with their quarter back 25-year-old Russell Wilson in only his second season whereas the Broncos in the experienced 37-year-old Peyton Manning had one of the greatest quarter backs in NFL history and a team with vast experience of both end of season games and playing in the Super Bowl itself. That Seattle Super Bowl win will surely lead other NFL teams to IBC as they now know that youth can triumph over experience.

2013/14: Premier League football

Manchester United had easily won the Premier League title in the 2012/13 season by 11 points, and as always their home record was first class, the best in the league, as they had won 16 of their 19 home games turning their Old Trafford ground with its 75,000 capacity crowds into a real fortress. However, as the new 2013/14 season started under their new manager David Moyes things were to change. After West Brom won 2-1 at Old Trafford in late September IBC set in big style as visiting managers felt that if West Brom could get a 'result' there then so could their team. As a result the fear of visiting the Old Trafford fortress and the expectation of defeat were replaced by a positive belief that United at home were vulnerable. This was exemplified by Everton's win on Dec 4th when their manager Roberto Martinez instead of bringing on defensive substitutes in the second half to ensure that a point would be achieved by 'shutting up shop' went for the win bringing on the creative Barcelona loanee Gerard Deulofeu and it worked as Everton won 1-0.

From 28th September to 16th March inclusive, with IBC clearly at work, Manchester United had a Premier League home record of PL 12 W 5 D 2 L 5, an average of 1.42 points per game compared to their average at home in PL games the previous season of 2.53 points per game. There can be little doubt that IBC played its part in getting David Moyes the sack!

1996: Lawn Tennis and the success of non-seeds

The 1996 Wimbledon Men's singles provided a classic example of IBC as after Andre Agassi's early shock exit one after another the seeded players were knocked out. After each non-seeded player won it clearly had a confidence boosting impact on the other non-seeded players with IBC definitely at work! The biggest 'shock' came when the hot favourite Pete Sampras was knocked out in the quarter-finals by Richard Krajicek in straight sets. So eventually with all the seeded players eliminated there was a final between two non-seeds when Richard Krajicek beat Malivai Washington in straight sets.

IBC 5: Comparisons with close friends and family
2003: Craig Stadler

A week after winning on the Seniors Tour, as it was then called, Craig Stadler kept his form to win the BC Open on the USPGA tour on 20th July. After that win 50-year-old Craig called his 49-year-old good friend Peter Jacobsen encouraging him to win the following week's tournament, The Greater Hartford Open, because if he did they would be paired together on the beautiful Hawaiian island of Maui in the 2004 season opening all winners event, The Mercedes Championship as they would have won in successive weeks. So with an added Hawaiian incentive IBC was at work big style in Connecticut as the 49-year-old 'Jake' won as a 250/1 rank outsider — it was his first win in 8 years!!

2013: Justin Rose

Scott's 2013 US Masters triumph was followed in the very next major by Justin Rose's win in the US Open. We have already discussed how the Funeral Factor motivation was of real significance that week for Justin nevertheless in his preparation for that tournament Justin, who was born within a fortnight of Adam and is a very close friend of the Australian, was inspired by Scotty's Augusta victory.

2014: Alexander Levy

Alexander Levy is a close friend of fellow Frenchman Victor Dubuisson who is the same age. Victor burst on to the golfing scene in late 2013 by winning the Turkish Airlines Open, following up the next week with third place at the DP World Tour Championship, and he then started 2014 with second place in the WGC Accenture World Match play to virtually secure his Ryder Cup place. So Alexander, inspired by his good friend, in just his second season on the European Tour, won for the first time when he triumphed in the China Open in late April after which he admitted that IBC had been at work. Indeed he said that it was not only himself who'd been inspired by his friend's achievements as 'Victor's performances over the last few months inspired all the French players'.

2014: Seung-Yul Noh

In May 2013 Sang-Moon Bae won for the first time on the USPGA Tour when he won the Byron Nelson Championship. In his final round his playing partner had been the American Keegan Bradley and that fact was remembered by Bae's close friend, and fellow South Korean, Seung-Yul Noh when he was leading by two shots after the third round in the 2014 Zurich Classic of New Orleans because he too was to play alongside Keegan Bradley in the final round. So Noh took IBC from the fact that his friend had won for the first time when partnered by Bradley so if he could do it Noh felt that he could do so too — and he did just that winning by two shots for his first victory on the USPGA tour.

2014: Nicholas Thompson inspired by his sister Lexi

Nic is a 31-year-old golfer who is still looking for his maiden win on the USPGA Tour while his 19-year-old sister Lexi plays on the LPGA, and she is a seriously good player who was the youngest ever winner on the LPGA Tour when she won the Navistar Classic when just 16 and 7 months, and three months later she also became the youngest ever winner of a ladies European Tour event when she won the Dubai Ladies Championship in December 2011.

In the 2014 USPGA season Nic had been in poor form missing the cut in 8 of his first 14 tournament starts in which he hadn't had a single top 25 finish. However, things were about to improve!! His sister Lexi on April 6th won the Kraft Nabisco Championship which is one of the Majors on the LPGA winning by 3 shots after a 64-69-68 finish and in so doing became the second youngest ever winner of a woman's major.

Nic was clearly inspired by his sister's performance as he produced his best golf of the season — at the same time as his sister was winning her first Major he finished 24th in the Shell Houston Open, and then in his next tournament, the RBC Heritage Classic, he started as a 200/1 outsider, played well for three days so he was T3rd starting the final round before finishing 12th. It was easily his best performance and highest finish of the season. So his two highest finishes of the season came in the two tournaments he played during and just after Lexi's major victory!! IBC sibling style rules OK!!

IBC strikes TWICE for star golfer Ian Woosnam

IBC with Gary Player

Ian is just 5 foot 4½ inches tall and although he had a powerful physique due to lifting heavy bales on the family farm he was small for a golfer. However, he knew that the legendary South African golfer Gary Player, who had won all the Golf Majors [nine in all] including three US Masters, was similar to himself as Gary was only 5 foot 6 inches — just an inch and a half taller than 'Woosie' who said on TV that 'Gary Player was a little guy playing against big guys', and also 'like me he didn't hit the ball a long way. He was a great inspiration to me.'

IBC with Sandy Lyle

'Woosie' was born a month after golfer Sandy Lyle and as they grew up they were rivals in Shropshire County golf as well as playing together for that County, Sandy went on to win the Open in 1985 and the US Masters in 1988 and the success of his former County buddy was to be a real inspiration to Ian. Indeed 'Woosie' has admitted that seeing another Shropshire lad winning at Augusta in 1988 was a big inspiration to him when he teed off in his fourth US Masters in 1991, and the rest, as they say, is history as Ian holed an 8 footer on the last to win.

Woosnam's Augusta triumph was to be both his first and his last major win. Nevertheless he became the World's No 1 player after that US Masters victory, a position he was to hold for 10 months. Fifteen years later Ian was the [winning] Ryder Cup captain at the K Club in 2006 and it was nice to see that he had appointed Sandy as one of his assistant captains.

So here we have a unique example of a **double use of IBC** enabling star golfer Ian Woosnam to know that it was possible for a short guy [Gary Player] like himself to be a world star, and he also knew that a Shropshire lad [Sandy Lyle] like him could win a major at Augusta.

Finally, before we assess IBC let's remember my favourite example that was in my third golf annual in 1996. It is funny, sad and revealing and it happened almost 20 years ago.

1995: One recovering alcoholic inspires another!

In 1995 senior golfer Brian Barnes took inspiration from John Daly's Open play-off win at St Andrews, after all if one ex-alcoholic could win why not another? Barnes often joked that the affect of his drinking was that when he stood on the tee he often saw three balls and when asked what he'd then do his reply was simple — 'I tried to hit the middle one!' Brian took inspiration from the Major win of ex-alcoholic John Daly and won the Seniors' British Open just a week after Daly's Open victory. 'This is amazing when you consider two and a half years ago I was on Skid Row, and John Daly is a recovering alcoholic and so am I.'

ASSESSMENT

The question now is how can we use what we have learned about IBC to analyse and forecast forthcoming sporting events?

IBC applied to golf

I first wrote about Inspiration By Comparison 18 years ago in my third golf annual for which the then sports editor of the Racing Post Derek McGovern wrote the foreword and in it Derek gave 'inspiration by comparison' as an example of my 'original ideas'. Since its introduction then it has become regularly used by golf tipsters and analysts notably by the legendary Jeremy Chapman, and also by Steve Palmer his successor as *Racing Post* golf analyst, while Ben Coley, David John and Dave Tindall in their first-class columns are serial users of the IBC concept so that today the impact that one golf winner can have on others is regularly used by analysts.

So I suggest after any tournament we ask, 'which players could be inspired by the winner?' Then consider any player with the same coach, any player in a similar age group, other player[s] who are friends of the winner, if the winner was posting his maiden win consider other players who have yet to win, and, of course any players from the same country as the winner.

Having identified any players who could be subject to IBC you can then see if any of our other secrets also apply to them. Is, for example, the Nappy Factor, a Landmark birthday, the Funeral Factor or any of the secrets such as Positive Mental Associations, players on the Comeback Trail, or Mental Let Down applicable? Of course more obvious factors such as current and course form must also be considered.

IBC in team sports

By its nature IBC applies more easily to individual than to team sports as a team, unless of course it's an international team, will, for example, often have players of different nationalities so IBC based on nationality is often impossible. Nevertheless IBC can be applied to team sports as we have seen in these four recent examples of

- Derby's reaction to their 2014 Championship defeat
- Bournemouth's climb up the Championship in 2014
- The 2014 Super Bowl win by Seattle Seahawks
- Man United's poor 2013/14 home Premier League form

So when a particular team wins or loses we can ask whether there is anything unusual about the result that could inspire other teams to success. For example did the winning team, like Seattle in the 2014 Super Bowl, place an emphasis on youth so other American football teams with a similar age structure might in future be subject to IBC. Perhaps the 'shock' home defeat of a top football team like Manchester United in 2013/14 showed a vulnerability that can inspire their future opponents, or as with Derby County a club can be inspired to recover from a devastating play off defeat by the example of two other clubs who did just that. After Burnley's 2014 promotion to the Premier League every small club in the Championship will be using IBC as they strive to emulate the Lancashire club.

CHAPTER EIGHT
MENTAL LET DOWN

I introduced the concept of Mental Let Down 20 years ago in my first Golf Book when in relation to golf I wrote that, 'Mental Let Down refers to the likelihood that after a victory although obviously confident and in form a player may actually feel drained. He may have gone 'over the top' mentally to such an extent that just four days later in the following tournament he simply cannot get back into that 'zone' again. Let's always remember the enormous mental strain of playing when in serious contention.'

The essence of MLD was that after a win there would probably be a reduction in mental energy so MLD would occur immediately AFTER a victory. However, when analysing sporting performance we can now extend the use of this powerful concept in FOUR important ways.

- MLD can apply WITHIN a golf, tennis, or snooker tournament and within a football match
- MLD can be extended to sports other than golf where it can strike AFTER an important win.
- MLD can be extended to apply to the SEASON after a very successful season
- MLD can also occur after a FAILURE.

So let's start by looking at SIXTEEN examples from THREE different sports of MLD happening WITHIN a tournament or match.

Jimmy White in the 1992 World Snooker Championship Final
When the winning line is in sight a sportsman can start to think of what he'll say to the media after his victory, and how his win will affect his personal and sporting life as it will certainly result in a big cheque and a huge rise in the world rankings. Such thoughts may be difficult to contain as the player 'gets ahead of himself' and so 'gets in his own way' with such premature thoughts that then create a loss of focus, loss of concentration and before he knows it the loss of his winning position. It is very rare for a player to admit to this although we do have one classic, if sad, example.

Jimmy White is one of the most naturally skillful snooker players of all time. However, he has never won the World Snooker Championship although he has been in the final six times. However, the 1992 Final against Stephen Hendry was the one that really got away because 'The Peoples' Champion' Jimmy had built a 14 frames to 8 lead, and with a possible 13 frames left he needed to win just 4 more frames to become the World Champion. At that point Jimmy recalls that he lost his concentration on the match. 'Sitting in my seat I was literally thinking who I was going to thank, who I'm not going to thank. All of a sudden I sort of completely collapsed.' And collapse he did losing 10 consecutive frames to lose the final 18-14!

Golf: The inaugural 2014 Eurasia Cup

Here we have a similar example in a different sport when a team also suffered from MLD when, like Jimmy White, they also seemed certain to win.

The Eurasia Cup event was introduced to the golfing schedule in March 2014. It is played between two teams representing Europe and Asia and the inaugural contest was played at the Glenmarie Golf and Country Club in Kuala Lumpur, Malaysia. It is similar to the Ryder Cup although in this event there are just 10 players including a playing captain in each team, and all the players play in every session over its three-day duration.

In the pre-tournament betting the heavy hitters 'lumped on' Europe to win and they were backed in from an initial 8/15 to 2/5 as they had the better players with much higher world rankings than the members of the Asian team so the result looked a foregone conclusion. Indeed after the European team won all five four-ball matches by at least a two hole margin on Thursday to take a 5-0 lead it was 'obvious' that Europe did have much the stronger team and were 'certain' to win. Put simply after that first day 'mauling' nobody on the planet gave the Asian team a chance!

However, MLD set in big style in the European team and as always with MLD it wasn't that the players didn't try, or didn't care it was just that subconsciously they'd 'switched' off. As superb TV commentator Jamie Spence said 'The players must have thought it was already in the bag'.

As a result the Asian team in the Friday foursomes won two, halved two, and lost one of the five matches to win that session 3-2.

Nevertheless they were still losing 7-3 when the singles started. That Saturday was to be a truly memorable day as the tournament that Europe had looked certain to win, went down to the final singles match on the final green on that final day. Asia won six of the singles, halved two and lost just two, and so by winning the singles 7-3 the match finished 10-10 — it was a tie! Over the final two days the European team suffering from MLD had lost both sessions, taken only one third of the points available and won only three of those final fifteen matches!

Golf 2013+2014: The 'Law of the Streaker'

In this third example of MLD within a tournament we stay with golf using two examples.

In my golf books I often referred to this 'Law'. It applied whenever a golfer had a 'streak' of low scoring as a result of which he posts a score probably in the low-mid sixties. However, the key point is that it is invariably followed by an ordinary round as the player suffers from MLD as he finds it really difficult the next day to repeat the streak of brilliance he showed just 24 hours earlier. He finds it virtually impossible to get 'in the zone' again especially as he then faces possible changes in the weather, in his playing partners, his tee time and in the pin positions.

In a later chapter we'll refer to the golfer Stephen Gallacher's Positive Mental Associations with the Dubai Desert Classic which the Scot won in both 2013 and 2014. For now let's examine his scorecards for this par 72 course over the last two years.

2013: **63** 70 **62** 71 total 266
2014: **66** 71 **63** 72 total 272

You can clearly see that 2014 is almost a mirror image of 2013 as in each year he had two outstanding low-scoring rounds, and in each year they were followed by two solid, but much higher scoring, rounds.

The average score for each round in the two years combined is
2013+2014: **64.5** 70.5 **62.5** 71.5

As you can see the average score for the second round is six more than for the opening round, and for the final round it averages nine more than for round three. The four brilliantly low rounds over the two years are in each case followed by significantly poorer rounds the next day.

However, the 'Law of the Streaker' is like all the 'Laws' in Sports Analysis a statement of tendency and unlike the Laws of Physics it is therefore not a law with universal application.

The exceptions will probably be when the course is playing very easy with the weather consistently dry and warm. Nevertheless MLD is always very likely after a very low round. Indeed in the first seven European Tour tournaments in 2014 the ten round one leaders, or joint leaders, averaged 64.9 yet in the second round, the very next day, they averaged only 72.4 — exactly seven and a half shots poorer.

October 9th 2014 — The putt for a 59 followed by Mental Let Down.
The 33-year-old Belgian Nicolas Colsaerts playing in the first round of the 2014 Portugal Masters missed a very makeable birdie putt for an historic round of 59 on the final hole of his opening round. In his second round starting on the 10th he was only one under par for his first 10 holes compared to being 8 under for the very same holes in round one!

The rain-ruined tournament was reduced to just 36 holes with the long hitting Colsaerts finishing 2nd.

As multiple winner and two time US Open champion Lee Janzen once said of the USPGA Tour that 'It's amazing how often guys on tour shoot seven or eight under one day, next day they shoot above par. It happens to everyone.'

Football — MLD can occur in two ways within a match.
The first is when a team suffers from MLD after building a big lead because there is always a danger that they think that they have already won and so as MLD sets in the lead can quickly disappear.

May 2005: The famous Istanbul Champions League Final

MLD played a huge part when Liverpool won the now legendary Istanbul 2005 Champions League Final. They were losing 3-0 to AC Milan at half-time at which point Jamie Carragher later admitted he just wanted to avoid a heavy embarrassing defeat. In the second half Milan relaxed thinking the game was won while inspired by Steven Gerrard Liverpool re-grouped, and fought back to force a 3-3 draw. Then they somehow survived extra time before winning the penalty shoot-out!

However, more recently we have seen fight backs in THREE top class matches one from an even bigger deficit and both in shorter time than the legendary Istanbul CL final.

February 2011: Arsenal lose a four goal lead in a Premier League game

It came in the Premier League on 5th February 2011 when Newcastle were playing Arsenal at St James' Park. Arsenal blitzed the home side and were 3-0 ahead after just 10 minutes and they led 4-0 at half time. Some home fans left fearing a real humiliation. However, with the game clearly 'won' Arsenal suffered a collective MLD. It was as if virtually the whole side had 'switched off'. They became complacent, and careless yet although they had Diaby sent off with 22 minutes remaining they still led 4-0. Then in a 15-minute spell a Leon Best strike sandwiched between two Joey Barton penalties made it 3-4 with seven minutes to play. The recovery was completed when a Cheike Tiote volley made the score 4-4. Newcastle had achieved their own 'Istanbul'.

May 5th 2014: Crystal Palace v Liverpool — Istanbul in reverse as Liverpool lose a three goal lead in just 12 minutes!

This was a game that Liverpool had to win to effectively keep alive their chance of winning the PL title. After Luis Suarez had scored to make it 3-0 in the 56th minute he rushed into the net to recover the ball as he wanted his side to press for more goals to reduce Man City's goal difference advantage. It was a tactic with which neither captain Steven Gerrard on the pitch nor manager Brendan Rogers off it seemed to disagree. As a result the game opened up nevertheless with 12 minutes to play although they looked shaky defensively Liverpool still held that three goal lead.

However, in those twelve minutes a deflected shot from Damien Delaney, and two goals from substitute Dwight Gayle turned the game 'on its head'. It ended 3-3, it was a reverse-Istanbul, and it was also effectively the end of Liverpool's title challenge. It was also a rare example of a team with MLD 'knowing it had won' trying to widen its victory margin!!

November 4th 2014: Arsenal are 'at it again' losing a three goal lead in a Champions League Group match

Arsenal at home to Anderlecht in a Champions League Group D game led 3-0 with just under half an hour to play. As the TV commentator said

'Surely now passage to the Knock out stages of the Champions League is just a matter of time', and that view was reflected in odds of 1,000/1 on for Arsenal to win!

However, two goals from Van Den Borre, and a diving header from Mitrovic in the dying seconds made it 3-3. After the match Arsene Wenger said that '**maybe** we lost our concentration thinking the job was done' while Oxlade-Chamberlain felt that '**maybe** there was a bit of complacency at 3 nil up'. Let's be clear there was no 'maybe' about it, this was another classic case of MLD in action!

Football — MLD that can follow after a goal has been scored

The second way in which MLD can strike within a football match is after a goal has been scored. The ecstatic feeling that can follow a goal can result in all sorts of uncontrolled celebrations, as well as the planned pre-arranged dances that have been rehearsed earlier in the week in training. However, it has always been true that a side is at its most vulnerable when it has just scored because in those crucial seconds before the non-scoring side restarts the game there is a massive danger that MLD has set in. The celebrating players have often 'switched off' as they've focused on their celebrations, they may not return to their team shape, they may 'lose' the opposing players they are supposed to mark, and so they are really vulnerable in those vital couple of minutes after their opponents have restarted the game.

2014 World Cup provided three Group stage examples

18th June — Group B — Australia v Holland

Holland took the lead after 20 minutes through Arjen Robben, and straight from the restart, just 13, yes just 13, seconds later, Tim Cahill with a world-class left-foot volley equalised. Holland went on to win 3-2

25th June — Group F — Argentina v Nigeria and Bosnia v Iran

Lionel Messi gave Argentina the lead in the third minute and just 70 seconds later Musa equalised for Nigeria so it was 1-1 after 4 minutes! Argentina went on to win 3-2.

Iran, trailing 2-0, scored after eighty two minutes yet within 60 seconds Bosnia had scored their 3rd goal to make it 3-1 which was how the game ended.

There were also classic examples in three top class matches in three different leagues in the last seven weeks of the 2013/14 football season.

12th March 2014 — Championship — Birmingham v Burnley

Michael Duff had scored for Burnley in the 67th minute to give his team a 2-1 lead. However, within 80 seconds Birmingham had equalised with a goal from Emyr Huws and as Matt Murray, the Sky commentator on that game, said 'It's amazing how many times a team score and then go and concede.' The game ended 3-3.

9th April 2014 — Champions League quarter-final 2nd leg — Bayern Munich v Manchester United [first leg 1-1]

With 56 minutes gone and the score 0-0 Manchester United scored a crucial away goal when left back Patrice Evra rocketed a 25-yarder into the net. United's players celebrated big style. However, their joy was short-lived as just 22 seconds after the restart Bayern had equalised!! The commentator said, 'United were still celebrating their goal' and 'it was a schoolboy error' which was very unfair to schoolboys! It was also particularly fitting that although several United players were culpable the main culprit was their goalscorer Evra who had 'lost' his man for that equalising goal. Bayern went on to win 3-1.

19th April 2014 — Premier League — Tottenham Hotspur v Fulham

Spurs opened the scoring after 36 minutes when Paulhino converted from a superb Eriksen free kick. However, within 100 seconds Fulham's star midfielder Steve Sidwell had burst through Spurs' Fryers-Kabul centre-back combination to equalise. As BT commentator Michael Owen said it was a, 'perfect illustration of the old adage that you score one and you concede one so soon after.' Spurs went on to win 3-1.

There were two further classic examples in the opening months of the 2014/15 football season.

30th September 2014 — Champions League Group game — Paris St Germain v Barcelona

PSG took the lead with a goal from their newly signed centre back David Luiz. From the restart Barca equalized after some brilliant inter-passing was finished perfectly by Lionel Messi, and no surprise that PSG goal scorer David Luiz was at fault. As commentator Jon Champion observed 'It's a wonderful goal. Barca were behind for barely a minute'. PSG won the match 3-2.

5th October 2014 — Premier League — Leicester City v Burnley.

Newly promoted Burnley went into this match with just one away point from their first three PL games in which they hadn't scored a single goal. So when Michael Kightly gave them the lead in the 39th minute there was understandable joy and relief as they celebrated scoring their first PL away goal. However, MLD set in and within a minute Mahrez had equalized for Leicester. The match finished 2-2.

October 14th 2014 saw two further examples of how the nature of a celebration can lead to defeat, and even DEATH!

European Under-21 international Championship play-off second leg — Sweden v France. [First leg France won 2-0]

This was a vital game as the winners would qualify for the U21s finals in 2015.

France were 3-0 down with 3 mInutes to play when defender Layvin Kurzawa scored to make it 3-1 which, with the away goals rule, would see France through to the 2015 finals. After scoring the goal Kurzawa taunted the Swedish players, especially their striker John Guidetti, with a salute celebration. Almost immediately Sweden equalized when Oscar Lewicki scored his second goal of the match to give the home team a 4-1 win and a place in the 2015 Finals. After that decisive goal the Swedes retaliated by using the same taunting salute celebration that had just been used against them by France.

So here we have a unique example of a team not only celebrating but doing so in a provocative manner that was certain to lead to MLD for themselves and increased motivation for their opponents!

Indian league football — Bethlehem Vengthlang v Chanmari West
We have just seen a unique example of a provocative form of celebration involving a taunting salute and how it led to defeat! Now we have a unique, and I hope never to be repeated, example that occurred on the very same day of a celebration that led to death! Peter Blaksangzuala scored for Bethlehem in this match and celebrated by doing several backward somersaults. Tragically he landed very awkwardly doing massive damage to his spinal cord and died from his injuries five days later.

FINALLY, WHY ARE TEAMS APPARENTLY SO UNAWARE OF POST GOAL MLD?

Are the modern millionaire players so precious that they must be allowed to over celebrate during a match? We know that players can control their emotions after they have scored as we regularly see players refusing to celebrate if they score against their former club. So if directed to reduce celebrations to a minimum would they really be so upset? The time to really celebrate should surely be the end of the game when victory has actually been achieved?

MLD can strike in the match or tournament STRAIGHT AFTER an important victory. Here we examine THREE examples from TWO different sports.
Football teams can be really vulnerable in the match following a really significant win. Two instances of this stand out in the football season that ended in May 2014.

April 2014 — Leicester City after they had clinched promotion to the Premier League
After a superb unbeaten run in the Championship throughout 2014 — PL 16 W 11 D5 — Leicester City, although not playing that day, were promoted to the Premier League on Saturday 5th April. The bonuses had been won, the party had started, and the players had relaxed. However, Leicester

were to play Brighton at home in a Championship match just three days later on Tuesday evening. Let's remember that, although Brighton were chasing a play-off place, Leicester hadn't lost a league game all calendar year yet as you'd expect, Leicester suffered from MLD big style losing that home match 4-1!!

November 2013 — Arsenal after two wins to nil in big games suffer MLD at Old Trafford

The Gunners had beaten Liverpool 2-0 at home in the Premier League on Saturday 2nd November, and then in midweek they'd travelled to Germany beating Borussia Dortmund 1-0 in the Champions League. Those two wins led to forecasts that Arsenal could go 'all the way' in the Champions League and as they were leading the Premier League they would also be serious contenders for that big domestic prize.

They then faced their third really 'massive' game in eight days on Sunday November 10th when they played Man. United at Old Trafford in the Premier League. On the morning of the game the four journalists on the Sky TV's Sunday Supplement discussed the match yet none of them mentioned that Arsenal would be mentally drained after the two big games they had played that week as well as being tired by the travelling involved.

Former Arsenal striker Robin Van Persie had said before the match that 'We can't afford to lose'. So we had a motivated United team playing at home against a mentally drained Arsenal side. No surprise then that United won 1-0, so beating Arsenal by a single goal margin for the 4th time in their last five Old Trafford Premier League meetings. Admittedly other factors such as the late withdrawal of Arsenal centre back Mertesacker may have played a part. However, after watching Arsenal's superb win in midweek in Dortmund it was very clear that MLD was always going to be a key factor working against Arsenal's chance in that match.

Golf — MLD ensures that back-to-back wins are very rare

You'll recall that when I first wrote about MLD in my first golf book 20 years ago it was in the context of a professional golfer finding it extremely difficult after a win to play again just four days later in the next scheduled tournament and to win again. There is enormous mental pressure on any golfer in contention with a serious chance of winning a tournament and this is especially true of a golfer seeking that elusive, and always life changing, first win So once a win has been achieved there is for any golfer, especially for a first time winner, a huge MLD as it inevitably takes time to readjust, refocus and re-energise as well as adapting to the media attention that inevitably follows.

Let's look at the results on the European and USPGA tours over a period of five years from January 2010 to the end of the 2014 season.

The European Tour

On The European Tour there have been six instances of back-to-back winners

- 2010 Charl Schwartzel
  Africa Open and the Joburg Open in January

- 2011 Thomas Bjorn
  Johnnie Walker and European Masters in late August/early Sept

- 2011 Sergio Garcia
  Castello Masters and Andalucian Masters in late October

- 2012 Branden Grace
  Joburg Open and Volvo Golf Champions in January

- 2013 Brett Rumford
  Ballantines and the China Open in late April/early May.

- 2013 Phil Mickelson
  Scottish Open and the Open in July

All these players had won previously. 'Phil the Thrill' was a multiple US winner who had already won three Majors, Sergio Garcia had eight European Tour [ET] and seven USPGA Tour wins, Charl Schwartzel and Brett Rumford each had three ET wins while Branden Grace had won on the South Africa Sunshine Tour.

The USPGA Tour

By contrast on the much more competitive USPGA Tour back-to-back wins have been achieved by only two players in the last five years.

- 2012 + 2014 Rory McIlroy
  Deutsche Bank and BMW Championships [2012]
  WGC Bridgestone and the USPGA [2014]

- 2014 Billy Horschel
  BMW Championship and the Tour Championship

In 2014 having already won the Open in July Rory in successive weeks in August went on to win the WGC Bridgestone and the USPGA. Two years earlier in 2012 he had already won both the Honda Classic in April and the USPGA in August before he went on to win the Deutsche Bank and the BMW in consecutive weeks in September.

You'll recall that in Chapter 2 on the Nappy Factor we referred to Billy Horschel who in September 2014 won the final two tournaments of the USPGA season with back-to-back wins in the BMW Championship and the Tour Championship. He had only won once before on the Tour when he was victorious in the 2013 Zurich Classic of New Orleans.

ASSESSMENT

So in that recent period of five years there wasn't a single first-time winner who won back-to-back, and overall eight players won back-to-back with six of the eight already multiple winners.

It therefore seems fair to conclude that MLD is so powerful that back-to-back golf wins will rarely happen but when one does it is more likely to occur on the European rather than on the USPGA Tour, and by a player who is already a proven winner.

MLD can also be important THE SEASON AFTER a major success

In very recent years there have been FIVE interesting examples from FOUR different sports.

Golf — Players suffer MLD in the season after they've won the mega-lucrative FedEx Cup on the USPGA Tour

The FedEx Cup is a season-long points chase in which players can accumulate points in every USPGA tournament they play. The biggest tournaments like the four majors carry the most points. The top 125 points scorers over the season qualify to play in late August/early September in the FedEx Cup play-offs when in consecutive weeks the number is reduced to the top 100, then top 70 and finally to the top 30 who play in the season-ending Tour Championship. The FedEx Cup winner, on top of the monies he has won in the tournaments, takes home a tasty $10 million so whoever wins will have had a really successful season, and he'll also have shot up the world rankings. Plus, he will have a really happy bank manager!!

The danger is that such a player will suffer from MLD the following year as he has expended so much emotional energy into becoming the Fedex Cup winner that he will be so drained that he will find it difficult to rediscover the incentive, drive, and focus especially in the early months. As a result he will be unable to play anywhere near the standard of his winning year.

Let's look at the form of the last four Fedex Cup winners in the season after their mega success.

Winner in 2010 — Jim Furyk

In 2011 Slim Jim posted just two top tens, and one top twenty finish, and he didn't reach the season ending 30 man Tour Championship.

Winner in 2011 — Bill Haas

In 2012 after a sound start to the year with a win and a T4th finish Bill didn't post a single top ten finish from March to August during which time he had 4 missed cuts and only one top 25 finish in 10 starts

Winner in 2012 — Brandt Snedeker

In 2013 'Sneds' maintained his form really well starting the year with form figs of 3-23-T2-2 before he won the AT+T at Pebble Beach. Later in the year he also won the Canadian Open and ended a second consecutive successful year with five top 3 finishes including those two wins, and he'd won over £5.3million! No doubt at all there was no MLD for Snedeker.

Winner in 2013 — Henrik Stenson
Early in 2014 the Swede couldn't recapture the tremendous form he'd shown in the second half of 2013 so although he was playing steady golf and was making cuts he posted only one top ten finish in his first seven starts to May 12th, and his stats to that date showed how MLD had affected him as he was only 66th for Greens in Regulation and 72nd on the All-round stats compared to being 1st and 5th respectively in 2013.

Winner in 2014 — Billy Horschel
Billy has played in three tournaments since he lifted the Fedex Cup. He missed the cut in the Shriners Tournament, before he played in two limited field events — finishing T37th of 78 in the CIMB Classic, and T73rd of 80 in the WGC/HSBC. It is early to be definite however, it does seem clear from those poor performances that MLD is hitting Billy hard!

ASSESSMENT
It seems clear that MLD did set in with four of the five players although it certainly didn't with one of them.

The exceptional Brandt Snedeker
Brandt was already the father of a daughter when in 2012 his second child and first son Austin was born and you'll recall from Chapter 2 that this 'second child — first son' can be a highly motivating example of the Nappy Factor at work. So it could well be that in Snedeker's case MLD was wiped out by the Nappy Factor so enabling him to continue in 2013 with the superb form that brought him the Fedex Cup the previous year.

Rugby Union — The British Lions players suffer MLD in the season after their four yearly overseas tour
The British Lions tour every four years with the squad made up of the very best players drawn from the home countries of Ireland, Wales, Scotland and England. So this is a squad who only play together once when they visit either New Zealand, Australia, or South Africa on a four year rota. When they return home and return to their own countries they will then play in the Six Nations Championship which also includes France [and Italy] whose players were not on the Lions Tour.

With Rugby Union players immensely proud of becoming a British Lion the Tour is a real highpoint in any player's career so all players give it 100%. As a result they may often return home suffering from MLD as they are not only physically tired but emotionally drained when the new season's Six Nations Championship starts. On the other hand the French players are not so affected and therefore at an advantage when the Six Nations starts.

So if there is anything in this you would expect France to do especially well every four years in the Six Nations that comes straight after the Lions players have returned home. The last 16 Six Nations Champions are shown below with the winners shown after a Lions Tour highlighted. If there was a 'Grand Slam' when the Champions beat all the other Nations it is also shown

1998	**France**	**Grand Slam**
1999	Scotland	
2000	England	
2001	England	
2002	**France**	**Grand Slam**
2003	England	
2004	France	
2005	Wales	
2006	**France**	
2007	France	
2008	Wales	
2009	Ireland	
2010	**France**	**Grand Slam**
2011	England	
2012	Wales	
2013	Wales	
2014	**Ireland**	

As you can see France won the Six Nations Championship in 1998, 2002, 2006 and 2010 all of which came after Lions' tour years. However, they didn't win the title in 2014, the last post Lions tour year.

So that record of an 80% strike rate of French success in the years after a Lions tour suggests that it may well be true that France have an advantage in those years because unlike the four home countries they had no players suffering from post-Lions Tour MLD.

It may also be significant that four of France's six championship wins came in those four post Lions Tour wins.

However, it may be that irrespective of any Lions tours the French would have won the titles in 1998, 2002, 2006 and 2010 simply because they had the best team in each of those four years. Let's also remember that we are looking at a sample size of just five years.

Overall it's probably fair to say that this unusual application of MLD has some real substance.

Football 2013/14: MLD hits Old Trafford in the season after 'Fergie' leaves

After 'Sir' had retired from Manchester United at the end of the 2012/13 season it was always clear that the following season would be difficult as United had enjoyed unrivalled success in the previous two decades and had just won the Premier League by 11 points.

'Fergie' had built a fearsome reputation highlighted by his famous 'hairdryer' treatment as over 25 years he had built a club that was automatically every year in the Champions League and always challenging for or winning the Premier League title. So when David Moyes was 'annointed' by Sir Alex as his 'chosen one' it was hoped that there would be an almost seamless transition. In fact after a troubled season on the pitch, and with the club's share price falling David Moyes was sacked before United's troubled season, which we have already referred to in the IBC Chapter, ended.

However, one of the key elements was simply MLD as so many players consciously or subconsciously relaxed as the 'pressure' was off, the 'hairdryer' was nowhere to be seen, and some of the senior players admitted later that they were not at all impressed by their new manager. Indeed after United had won at Newcastle on April 5th 2014 Patrice Evra made a startling admission, although it was one I'd long suspected, when he said, 'In the Champions League we have played good, we are confident and it looks like we are up for it more than in the league and cup. I know it's not professional to say that, but it's the truth.' Wow — what an admission! Put simply the players were targeting the 'big' games especially the European games on the 'big stage'. Even a hint of that attitude would in previous years have seen 'the hairdryer in overdrive' as 'Sir' would have gone apoplectic! To the ordinary working man or woman the notion that you'll work hard some days but not others would seem alien and certainly when some United players earn more in a day than many workers earn in a year they would not expect players to pick and choose when they are 'up for it'.

So one factor in United's poor post 'Fergie' season was certainly Mental Let Down. Good title-winning senior players didn't become bad players overnight but they did reduce their levels of intensity, focus, and determination. It was as if there had been an almost collective sigh of relief as the new post-Fergie era started. Indeed as Evra said the players' appetite for continued success that had always been part of the 'United way', was only to be seen consistently in 'big' games and on those European nights.

Football — Autumn 2014 — MLD hits World Cup winners Germany when they start their Euro 2016 qualifying campaign.
Having won the World Cup in July Germany were expected to easily top their qualifying Group for Euro 2016. However, as 2014 ended they were only 3rd in their Group after playing 4 group games with only one away from home. Their campaign started with a fortunate 2-1 home win against Scotland before in their next two games they lost 2-0 in Poland before they drew 1-1 at home to Republic of Ireland. The German media were highly critical with Tagesspiegel joking that the part timers of Gibraltar would fancy their chances against the World Cup holders in the final Euro 2016 Q. match of the year! Germany won that match but only 4-0 when a bigger

win was both expected and required to boost the German goal difference. Overall it has been very clear that Germany was suffering from MLD. Yet surely that had to be expected after their Brazilian triumph!

POST-OLYMPIC LET DOWN
Cycling 2008 — Victoria Pendleton — 'when you win you suddenly feel lost'.
In Chapter One we noted that cyclist Victoria Pendleton, after her failure to win any medal in Athens in 2004 went on to win gold in Beijing four years later after successfully working with Dr. Steve Peters. However, her reaction to that tremendous triumph told us so much about MLD as she said 'It's almost easier to come second because you have something to aim for when you finish. When you win, you suddenly feel lost'.

Diving 2012+ — Tom Daley
In Chapter Six we noted how after the 2012 London Olympic 10-metre platform diving bronze medalist Tom Daley had admitted that he suffered a post-Olympic let down and how that had led to his poor subsequent form especially in 2014.

It is hardly surprising that after such an intensive pre-Olympic training programme so many athletes across a range of sports have suffered from similar strong feelings of MLD. Tom was by no means the first and he'll certainly not be the last to suffer in that way.

MLD can also occur AFTER FAILURE
We have seen how MLD can follow after success. However, it can also occur after a failure.

There is one sport which measures players' ability to recover from failure, and there are two interesting examples, one an individual and one a team, of MLD after failure.

Golf — the bounce back factor
The ability to handle disappointment is one of life's great skills and it's certainly vital to any sportsman. This is especially true in golf and on the USPGA Tour they have a statistic, called bounce back, which measures a player's ability to recover at once from playing a hole badly. So it measures in percentage terms how often a player is over par on a hole and then under par on the following hole. This stat can be a bit misleading if a player happens to make an error before playing a relatively easy hole compared to another player who makes his mistake before the toughest hole on the course. Nevertheless over a season the 'bounce back' stats can be revealing. At the end of the 2014 season

- Luke Donald was 1st at 27.39%
- Matt Kuchar was 152nd at 16.59%
- Ernie Els was 159th at 15.79%

Luke Donald's top place is not surprising as he's always had a cool temperament. However, it is surprising to see 'Kooch' who was world ranked 9th at the end of the 2014 season so lowly placed while it's sad to see 45-year-old four time Major winner Ernie Els in an even lower position!

Bernhard Langer's classic example of how to defeat MLD

The 1991 Ryder Cup played at Kiawah Island, South Carolina was known as the 'War on the Shore' because of the ultra- patriotic American crowds. At the end of the final day the result depended on just one match between the German Bernhard Langer and the American Hale Irwin. On the final green Langer faced a 6 foot putt knowing that if he holed it he would have beaten Hale Irwin and Europe would have drawn 14-14 and so, as holders, would retain the Ryder Cup, and that if he missed it the USA would regain the Trophy. The ball stayed above ground, Europe had lost, and the patriotic crowd went wild. Langer's name would forever be remembered for that failure so for 99.99% of golfers, missing that putt would have had a hugely devastating effect.

Mentally exhausted with the feeling that you personally had let your team down most golfers in Langer's situation would need to 'hide' by taking time to recover from such a massively draining experience. Yet as we discovered in the God Squad chapter Bernhard was a born again Christian so 'by having an eternal perspective and a personal relationship with Christ I was able to cope with it' as he proved the very next week when he returned to his native Germany to win the German Masters by holing a 15 foot putt to win a play off!! I make no apology for using an example that is almost a quarter of a century old yet it is still the very best example I have ever come across of any individual beating MLD so emphatically!

Liverpool–MLD would surely hit Anfield in the 2014/15 season?

Liverpool started the 2013/14 season as 33/1 outsiders to win the Premier League and they deservedly received a lot of praise for scoring 101 league goals in finishing second. However, with three games to play they were 6-1 on favourites to win the league for the first time in 25 years. To be certain of the title in a two-week period they had to draw with Chelsea at home, beat Crystal Palace away, and then beat Newcastle at home.

However, instead of playing for a point at home to Chelsea they were 'suckered' into Mourhino's web and following Steven Gerrard's famous slip just inside his own half the Reds lost the vital first goal and went on to lose 2-0. Then at Selhurst Park, as we have already seen, they threw away a 3-0 lead in the last 12 minutes against Palace by attacking rather than settling to control the game, and run the clock down.

On that last day at home to Newcastle Liverpool were 'flat' as MLD had set in and, although they recovered from being 1-0 down at half time to win 2-1, they were a shadow of the team that had set the league alight weeks before. On that final day they were 20/1, not 1/6, to win the title with

Man City 'sure' to get the single point they needed at home to West Ham. The final day 'celebrations' at Anfield were understandably very muted as everyone realised that a massive chance to lift the title had gone, and would probably not return for a long time.

Yes Liverpool had a season that exceeded expectations yet without a shred of doubt in those final two weeks Liverpool let an historic opportunity to win their first ever Premier League title slip through their fingers when they already had one hand on the trophy!

After such massive disappointment the 2014/15 season would almost inevitably start with a large element of MLD both for the club and its captain Steven Gerrard. Add in the sale of Suarez, Sturridge out injured from August, and several new signings to be blended into an enlarged squad and the new 2014/15 season was always going to be difficult for Liverpool, and so it proved. On Xmas Day 2014 although they had reached the Semi Final of the Capital One Cup they had been eliminated from the Champions League at the Group stage and were a disappointing 10th in the Premier League.

ASSESSING MLD
Let's bury 'After the Lord Mayor's show'
When I first wrote about MLD 20 years ago the idea that it was not easy to follow one good performance with another was often referred to as 'After the Lord Mayor's show' [ATLMS]. Today that dated phrase has little or no meaning to younger generations who have never seen and possibly never even heard of a Lord Mayor's Show, and, unlike MLD it cannot be applied within a tournament or match, or to the season following a successful season, and it can't be applied after failure. So let's now bury the dated and very limited old ATLMS.

On the other hand, as we have seen, MLD is a powerful, dynamic, versatile multi-use concept with several applications that can really help us in sports analysis, and especially in making sporting predictions.

MLD Vs CONFIDENCE
However, the key debate about the specific use of MLD after any success is how do we decide the balance between two possible alternative and conflicting forces? First there is the positive impact in boosting confidence and providing a real sense of momentum that success can bring. On the other hand, as a result of the process of focus, concentration, and 'being in the zone' that is required for victory the feeling after success can be one of being mentally exhausted, emotionally drained, as if 'your batteries' are all flat. Put simply — it's MLD versus Confidence.

My view is that so often today sportsmen have been advised by their PR people that they must appear confident and positive, and so a positive image is so often created, and it is that image that we tend to see and believe. We don't tend to look for and focus on the mental side of success. So let's return for a moment to that Manchester United v Arsenal Premier League match in November 2013, after which one headline read, 'Why did it take so long for Arsenal to get going?' The answer was simple — MLD. Yet all the pre match media focus was on the confidence that Arsenal had after their two wins to nil in the previous two games with no mention of the MLD they would inevitably feel at Old Trafford.

MLD and 'shock' results — not 'being up for it' is simply MLD in other words

Whenever there is an unexpected 'flat' team or individual performance it is so often caused by MLD.

As we have seen, Patrice Evra admitted a team may simply not be 'up for it', and not being 'up for it' is simply MLD in different words. Football teams can lack mental energy, mental focus and so suffer MLD and not be 'up for it' for 4 key reasons.

1. As in the classic example we have already looked at when Arsenal in November 2013, after two big wins in four days in the Premier League and Champions League, were mentally drained when three days later they went to Old Trafford and were beaten by Man. Utd.

2. A team is playing a lesser side they are expected to beat. This can happen when a team in one of the top positions plays against a team struggling towards the bottom of the table.

3. The players know that the match is low on the club's priorities. This is often the case with many PL clubs when playing in the Capital One Cup especially in the early rounds.

4. The 'Cyclops' Factor. Cyclops in Greek mythology was a Giant with just one big eye in his forehead. So the 'Cyclops Factor' refers to any team which when facing any game have 'a big eye' on what is a much more important match a few days later. This can happen for example when clubs play an 'ordinary' Premier League game just a few days before a crucial mid-week match in the Champions League.

Overall I'm convinced that MLD is one of the strongest weapons in the punters' armoury in the battle against the Bookies!

So whenever you are analysing any completed sports event ask whether an individual or team involved is likely to suffer MLD and to what extent?

And if analyzing a forthcoming match, or tournament, or even a season also think in terms of whether MLD is in any way relevant.

Discover more Sports Analysis Secrets at elliottsportanalysis.co.uk

CHAPTER NINE
THE COMEBACK TRAIL

Let's start by looking at when and how this concept was born, its early success as a predictor of sporting achievement, and how it's been developed before looking at TWELVE examples from 2013-2014 of the Comeback Trail in action covering five sports — football, national hunt racing, rugby union, golf and cricket.

THE BIRTH OF THE COMEBACK TRAIL TWENTY YEARS AGO

I introduced this concept in my very first golf book in 1994. It was based on the observation that golfers can lose form because of illness or injury, so a player with a track record of success can play poorly and spend one, two, maybe more years in the 'doldrums'. However, once such a player with a previous sound career record overcomes illness, or recovers from injury, he is on the Comeback Trail, and he was given the CT symbol in his player profile and such a rededicated, refocused, and refreshed player will have increased incentive, increased commitment, and an increased desire to succeed.

Peter Jacobsen

One example I then gave was of five time winning golfer Peter Jacobsen who had played poorly in 1993 and 1994. However, over the winter of 1994/95 he worked extremely hard on a fitness programme, used a psychologist, and spent a lot of time practising. So when the 1995 season started, although he hadn't posted a top 4 finish in the previous three years he was rarin' to go. He started on the Comeback Trail in February with two wins as he won the AT+T at 100/1 and followed up the very next week in the Buick Invitational at 40/1. Today you will see the personable 60-year-old 'Jake' working as an analyst for the Golf Channel and NBC covering the American USPGA Tour.

Jacobson's renaissance had convinced me that the Comeback Trail [CT] was a very important and potentially profitable concept. So in my second book I predicted that three American golfers, Steve Jones, John Cook, and Scott Verplank were worth following in 1996 as they were all on the CT.

Scott Verplank didn't play well in 1996 but the other two certainly did!

Steve Jones

Jones had won four times before his career was seriously derailed by a dirt bike accident after which he couldn't grip a club. That injury kept him from playing until he rejoined the tour on a medical exemption in 1994. He started to show improved form in 1995 with two top five finishes so he looked a sound choice as a player likely to win on the Comeback Trail in 1996, and so it proved. He posted three top ten finishes and was tied second in the AT+T when that tournament was voided at halfway so he was in solid form by mid-year when he prequalified for the 1996 US Open which he went on to win as a 150/1 outsider. A major win for a class player on the Comeback Trail!

John Cook

Cook was 3rd on the Money List in 1992 after three wins and a 2nd place in the Open. However, he then decided to remodel his swing which led to a serious dip in his form shown by his declining position on the Money List — from 2nd in 1992 to 37th 1993, 45th 1994 and a career low 97th in 1995. Although a six time winner he'd been without a win in three years so he looked to be just the sort of player to successfully hit the Comeback Trail in 1996 and he did just that winning the FedEx St Jude Classic at 28/1, and the CVS Charity Classic at 20/1.

THE DEVELOPMENT OF THE COMEBACK TRAIL CONCEPT

The examples of Peter Jacobsen, Steve Jones and John Cook proved that the Comeback Trail concept was one of real value as it focused on sportsmen with heightened motivation.

As originally conceived the CT applied only after injury or illness for a period of one maybe more years, and it applied to just one sport, golf. However, the exciting thing is that this important analytical tool can be developed in FOUR key ways.

First, the Comeback can take place after a sportsman has had a problem period that may have lasted from a short period of say a month to longer periods of a few years.

Second, the period of 'failure' preceding the comeback can be caused by many factors apart from injury or ill health, and I have identified eight all of which are illustrated in the eleven examples that follow.

Third, it is applicable to several sports and we'll look at recent individual examples from National Hunt horse racing, Rugby Union, Football, Cricket, as well as Golf.

Fourth, it can also be applied to teams as well as to individuals.

The application of the Comeback Trail to different time periods

The essence of the CT concept was that, after a 'problem period' of failure of a year or more, a proven sportsman will then have extra focus, extra determination and extra commitment as he strives to return to his previous good results and high levels of performance. Although when originally conceived the CT was solely applicable to comebacks after a year or more of failure it can be applied to FOUR different time periods.

Length of time after the period of 'failure' when the comeback can start

Short term	Up to six months after a period of 'failure'
Medium term	Starts six months to a year after the slump

Long term   One-two years before comeback starts
Very long term   A period of over two years

The very long term is the one used with Steve Jones and John Cook when the concept started.

The different problems that create the background for a comeback
There are probably EIGHT reasons that can lie behind a slump in the form of a previously successful sportsman.

- Financial problems due to ill-advised investments, tax problems, or divorce settlements

- Marital, family, or other relationship problems

- Lifestyle problems

- Difficulties with the player's agent, coach, or management company

- Changing equipment

- Problems regarding retainers and contracts

- Disciplinary issues

- Returning after regretting an earlier decision to retire.

THE COMEBACK TRAIL IN ACTION
Let's now look at TWELVE examples from 2013-2014 that cover FIVE sports, comebacks over different time periods, and include examples of all the above eight factors that can cause the initial period of failure. They also include a sportsman who has actually successfully hit the comeback trail TWICE in his career!!

2014 Premier League: Kevin Nolan — after disciplinary problems led to two red cards and two suspensions
Kevin Nolan, the captain of Premier League club West Ham, was sent off at Anfield in a 4-1 Premier League defeat to Liverpool on Dec. 7th 2013 and having returned after a suspension he was again sent off on New Year's Day 2014 at Craven Cottage when Fulham beat the Hammers 2-1. As a result Nolan was again suspended, this time for four Premier League matches and with his club in the bottom three and staring relegation in the face he became deeply unpopular with both the fans and his manager Sam Allardyce. 'Big Sam' who had bought him in 2011 to captain the club was understandably upset saying that 'He's let everyone down including himself. Our captain was irresponsible, not just for today but for the future'. He was heavily fined by the club with Nolan facing the lowest point in his career.

    When he returned to play he was therefore most definitely on the Comeback Trail as he knew he owed his manager, his teammates and the fans big style, and what a comeback it was as highly motivated, responsible and disciplined he scored both goals in a 2-0 home win against Swansea, then both goals in a 2-0 win at Aston Villa, and notched one of his team's goals in their 3-1 home win against Southampton. So in his first four games back he'd scored five goals helping his team move well clear of the relegation places. As 'Big Sam' said 'He had a lot of time to reflect on what happened. For him it was about rolling his sleeves up and using those weeks to define himself and show everyone what he can really do. **He's comeback with a bang!'**

2014 National Hunt horse racing: Davy Russell — after being 'sacked'

Davy is a National Hunt jockey who was Champion Irish National Hunt jockey in 2013. He also held one of the most coveted jobs in his sport as he was the retained jockey for the highly successful Ireland based Gigginstown House Stud team so he had the first pick of their horses. However, all that was to change on 31st December 2013 at Punchestown when he was told by the Gigginstown boss Michael O'Leary, who runs Ryanair, that he was no longer to be the number one rider for their team. In blunt terms he'd effectively been 'sacked' yet although he could have argued, complained, hit the media with his views and so 'burned all his bridges' he decided in effect 'to bite his tongue', and accept the decision. That dignified controlled response was to have its reward later on a special Friday in March.

Exactly ten weeks to the day since his sacking, the long awaited National Hunt Olympics, otherwise known as the Cheltenham Festival meeting, started, however, this time Davy no longer had a free Ryanair flight! Although still disappointed by what had happened he was nevertheless looking forward to Cheltenham and was most definitely on the Comeback Trail as he was determined to prove that New Year's Eve decision was wrong. However, in the first three days he'd had three falls but no winners!

However, the Cheltenham Friday will live forever in Davy's memory!!! Jockey Bryan Cooper who was Davy's successor at Gigginstown had sustained a horrible leg injury and his absence meant that Michael O'Leary needed a replacement jockey so as there had been no bust-up, no row, and trustworthy Davy was available he was asked if he would ride that day for Gigginstown. He agreed and the day got off to a flier as Davy rode Tiger Roll to win the Triumph Hurdle and later he partnered another Gigginstown horse, Savello to win the Grand Annual. So he had ridden two big Festival winners on the same day for his former employer!

However, between those satisfying wins he rode 20/1 outsider Lord Windermere from a long way off the pace to win the biggest race of the meeting, the Gold Cup by a short head and then he survived a stewards' enquiry.

That final day had ended with Davy Russell, the Comeback King, riding two winners for his ex-employer as well as the Gold Cup winner — it was a 3,926/1 treble!

2013/14 Football: Emmanuelle Adebayor — after problems with the coach led to him being 'frozen out'

At the start of the 2013/14 season Spurs' striker Adebayor had returned to Togo following the death of his brother, and after his return his relationship with coach Andres Villas-Boas [AVB] completely broke down. As a result the tall striker was 'frozen out' so he had to train with the youth team players. Spurs' form in the first four months of the season had been poor and the 'final straw' came when Liverpool went to White Hart Lane on Sunday 15th December and, on live TV, they demolished Spurs 5-0. The fans sang 'You're getting sacked in the morning' and he was as AVB left the next day 'by mutual consent' with Tim Sherwood later that week appointed as Spurs' new head coach.

With Spurs finding goal scoring difficult Tim immediately decided to take Adebayor out of 'cold storage' and resurrect his career. The tall 29-year-old Togo international striker was a player who was clearly on the Comeback Trail with a massive incentive to prove the departed AVB wrong, to prove he could still play well at the highest level, and to restore his reputation. And that's precisely what he did. His first game was a difficult Premier League match away at Southampton yet Spurs won 3-2 with Adebayor 'on fire' scoring twice to earn the 'Man of the Match' award. He went on to score four in his first five games, and he ended the season as the club's top Premier League goal scorer with 11 goals in 21 games.

No surprise that when the news broke in early April that Tim Sherwood would be replaced at the end of the season the tall striker was clearly saddened saying that 'he gave me back my life. I'm very grateful and owe big thanks for that. I respect him as a manager and a footballer'.

2013/14 Football: Luis Suarez — after serious disciplinary problems

Liverpool's Luis Suarez had a 'bad boy' image initially as a result of the 8 match ban he received for racially abusing Man United's left back Patrice Evra in a Premier League game at Anfield in October 2011, followed by his apparent refusal to shake Evra's hand when the two teams met again in February 2012. Add in regular criticism for alleged diving and he was becoming 'public enemy Number One'. Nevertheless Liverpool supported him giving him a new long-term contract before the following season.

However, on 21st April 2013 at Anfield in a televised league match against Chelsea Suarez was involved in a biting incident with Chelsea full back Ivanovic. The 'bad boy' was at it again, and we were reminded that Suarez had been involved in another biting incident earlier in his career in Holland. This time the ban was for 10 matches, which meant that his suspension would include the opening five games of the 2013/14 season.

To make matters a lot worse, the following month Suarez said he wanted to leave the club because of the way the press treated him. However, manager Brendan Rogers stood firm, saying that Suarez had shown 'total disrespect' for the club amid reports suggesting that the striker was not allowed to train with the first team. Liverpool refused to sell him as he was under contract nevertheless it was one 'helluva' mess!!

Yet 12 months to the day since that infamous biting incident Liverpool were top of the Premier League with Suarez having scored 30 Premier League goals. Now that's one massive example of the Comeback Trail in action!

How did it happen? Well let's remember that Luis is a 'street' footballer with an infectious enthusiasm for the game, and once he realised that Liverpool would not allow him to leave he accepted the situation as he wanted to play, and so he became a highly motivated player who owed the club, the manager and the fans so much for the way they had supported him through 'his difficulties'. Indeed, as we saw in Chapter One, Dr. Steve Peters had been assisting the Liverpool players including Luis so the Uruguayan striker had mental skills support while on the Comeback Trail.

Just over five months after the biting incident he returned to Premier League action at Sunderland at the end of September 2013 and scored twice in a 3-1 Liverpool win. Afterwards Brendan Rogers said Luis was 'On top of the world' because, as we discussed in Chapter Two on the 'Nappy Factor', he'd become the father of a son for the first time just a few days before his return to Premier League action.

Suarez' amazing season resulted in him receiving both the PFA and the Sports Writers' Player of the Year awards, and with Liverpool finishing second in the Premier League the club would again be playing Champions League football the following season.

If Luis Suarez was a horse his breeding would surely read by Comeback Trail out of The Nappy Factor!

However, in the World Cup with a worldwide audience watching on 24th June Suarez was again involved in a biting incident when Uruguay met Italy in a final Group D match. A four month ban from all football activity followed with Suarez moving to Barcelona in July so in the new season the Uruguayan striker will once more be on the Comeback Trail, although this time he won't have The Nappy Factor or Dr. Steve Peters to help him!

So by mid-summer 2014 if Luis Suarez was a horse his breeding would surely have read by Another Nibble out of The World Cup.

2013/14 National Hunt horse racing: Ryan Mania and Leighton Aspell — after coming out of retirement.

The decision to retire for any one at any time is rarely easy because you then have to find a 'new' life, new uses for your new 'time rich' life, and perhaps above all 'new' friends. The sportsman, unless he's a golfer, will be retiring when young, probably in his 30s, with at least half his life ahead of him — what's he going to do with it? Facing that problem some return to their sport. Given the adage 'that you don't know what you've got till it's gone' they return with renewed vigour, renewed commitment and renewed motivation as they are on the Comeback Trail.

So let's look at two National Hunt jockeys who came out of retirement and amazingly went on to achieve the same headline grabbing success in consecutive years.

Ryan Mania

Ryan is a Scottish jump jockey who rode for Northern trainers Peter Monteith and then for Howard Johnson. However, Johnson lost his license at the end of 2011 as a result of which at 22 years of age Ryan decided to retire. However, as the winter months passed by he saw horses running, and often running well, that he used to ride. So, supported and encouraged by his agent Bruce Jeffrey, he decided to come out of retirement and, returning to the saddle, he started to ride for West Yorkshire trainer Sue Smith who had a staying handicap chaser in her yard called Auroras Encore who'd been bought by Sue's famous, former showjumping, husband Harvey Smith for just 9,500 guineas. Ryan got 'the leg up' on the horse to finish second in the 2012 Scottish Grand National after which the horse was trained for the 2013 Grand National. It was to be Ryan's first ever National ride and the 23-year-old, on the Comeback Trail after his earlier retirement, rode Sue Smith's bay gelding to a nine lengths victory! Sadly because of continuous problems with his weight Ryan announced his retirement for a second time on November 25th 2014 just 18 months after his Grand National triumph.

Leighton Aspell

In July 2007 Leighton announced his retirement from race riding. However, after 12 months he felt 'I had some unfinished business and after watching Cheltenham I realised how much I was missing it'. So, after an 18 month break the 33-year-old with support from Oliver Sherwood and Lucy Wadham, the trainers he used to ride for, successfully reapplied for his license, returned to the saddle, and to the buzz of the weighing-room that he'd missed so much.

With renewed enthusiasm Leighton re-launched his career, and he even had an official fan club formed in his honour started by a guy who backed a 66/1 winner that he'd steered to victory. He arrived at Aintree in early April 2014 in good form having ridden 60 winners with Pineau de Re his mount in the Grand National, and what a superb ride he gave the 11-year-old as he ensured that the horse didn't fall after errors at the 18th and at Bechers second time round. He'd ridden a brilliant race yet as he passed the post there was no fist pumping, no whoops of joy, no joyous whip waving as Leighton stayed cool, calm, and composed while inwardly overjoyed.

For the second successive year the world's most famous steeplechase had been won by a jockey on the Comeback Trail after retiring!!

2014 Cricket: Andrew 'Freddie' Flintoff — after coming out of retirement — 'It's a bit like sex, it's always better second time'
In early July 2014 five years after his last senior match 'Freddie' Flintoff came out of retirement to play for Lancashire in the Twenty20 Blast. Since his retirement 'Freddie' has been a darts commentator, a boxer, appeared on TV adverts, and become a 'celebrity' yet he'd clearly missed cricket and he wanted his children to see him play. His injury prone body will certainly prevent him from reaching the higher levels of the game again yet he's playing with a smile, and as he said, 'it's a bit like sex, it's always better the second time!'

However, so often we find that older sports stars who come out of retirement find that mentally and physically they simply can't repeat their earlier glories. A good example was Australian swimming ace Ian 'The Torpedo' Thorpe who retired in 2006 and coming out of retirement 5 years later he failed to make the Australian team for the 2012 London Olympics.

2014 Rugby Union: Danny Cipriani — after a lifestyle 'light bulb moment'
Danny is a Rugby Union player who has been on the Comeback Trail after an early career that was littered with controversy and bad headlines. On the eve of his England debut his 'inappropriate behaviour' led to him bring dropped from the squad. He won the first of his seven caps against Ireland in 2008 before coach Martin Johnson dropped him because he'd had enough of his behaviour and attitudes. Danny's England days were clearly over. He then moved to the newly formed Super 15 team Melbourne Rebels in Australia in 2010 where controversy followed him like a trusted spaniel before he returned to England to join Sale in 2012 and although he scored almost 200 first season points the club owner criticised his attitude. However, the defining moment seems to have been when he was hit by a bus on a team night out in Leeds at the end of his first season in 2013. That incident was to be the tipping point, a real 'light bulb moment' for the Sale fly-half.

After that Danny accepted that 'things had to change' and he started on the Comeback Trail at the start of the 2013/14 season. He fully accepted that first and foremost he is a Rugby Union player not a celebrity so he'd started to work regularly with motivational guru Steve Black, and overhauled his lifestyle to prevent the continual dramas of the past with a more carefully chosen circle of friends. On the field his performances were widely praised as in his position of fly-half he realised, now more than ever, that he had to make the right decisions for his team. His form had helped Sale finish 6th in the Premiership and so qualify for the Heineken Cup.

After five years of 'problems' when very young 26-year-old Danny by May 2014 was clearly a 'new' changed man and a 'new' changed player. His journey on the Comeback Trail led to his recall to the England training squad in May, followed by his selection for the early summer New Zealand tour in which, although not starting a test match, he played well off the bench in the games against the All Blacks in Auckland and Hamilton. So Danny's journey on the Comeback Trail had succeeded as he'd played for England again after a six-year absence!

2013 Golf: Henrik Stenson. The Comeback King for the second time after serious financial and health problems

Henrik was a very successful top class golfer who in the five years from 2005-2009 established himself as a world class player with four wins on the European Tour, and his first victory in America when he landed the prestigious 2009 Players' Championship after which he reached 5th place in the World rankings. However, later that year came the 'bombshell news' that he'd lost a very large part of his life savings in the Ponzi scheme run by the convicted fraudster Allen Stafford and subsequently his form dipped and he was then hit by a second blow when in November 2011 he contracted viral pneumonia as a result of which he lost a lot of physical strength. So by early 2012 the former world number 5 had seen his ranking fall to 230th!!

So working with his coach, Pete Cowen and his sports psychologist Torsten Hansson he set out on the Comeback Trail with his breakthrough win coming in November 2012 when on the European Tour he won the South African Open by three shots. It was his first win for three and a half years and it gave him a much needed confidence boost going into the New Year, and what a new year 2013 was to be for the tall Swede!

In the second half of 2013 Henrik was in 'the form of his life' as in America he won the lucrative FedEx Cup Series after winning the Deutsche Bank Championship and the Tour Championship, and he was also successful on the European Tour winning the season-ending DP World Tour Championship in Dubai and so he also won the Race to Dubai [R2D], and in so doing he became the first ever player to win the FedEx-R2D double. He also posted big finishes in the years' last two Majors with a 2nd in the Open, followed by a 3rd in the USPGA.

The interesting, if little-noticed thing, about Henrik is that this was the **second time in his career that he'd been on the Comeback Trail** as after his first European Tour win in the Benson and Hedges in May 2001 his form evaporated shown by the fact that from June to the end of 2001 he didn't post a single top 40 finish, and in 2002 he missed 14 cuts and couldn't finish inside the top 30. He later admitted 'they were very tough times', and the fact that he came through them to reach the 5th spot in the World must have acted as an inspiration to him when he faced the Comeback Trail for the second time.

2013/14 Golf: Rory McIlroy — after changing equipment suppliers and management companies

Rory is the 'kid' from Northern Ireland whose precocious talent saw him take the golf world by storm between 2010 and 2012. He had already announced himself when he won the 2009 Dubai Desert Classic as a 19-year-old and in the following year although winless he'd finished 3rd in two majors, the Open and the USPGA, and he scored two points for the winning European side in the 2010 Ryder Cup. Then within 24 months in 2011/12 he won two majors, the 2011 US Open, and the 2012 USPGA and he won them both by 8 shots!! He also won the 2012 Race to Dubai after he won the DP World Championship in Dubai and he'd played a key role scoring three points when the European Team retained the Ryder Cup in 'The Miracle at Medinah'.

Off the course Rory seemed settled with his girl-friend, the Danish star tennis player Caroline Wozniacki, and on course he was a two time major winner with a strong all round golf game who'd triumphed on both sides of the Atlantic. So as 2013 beckoned the likeable 23-year-old kid with the ready smile, the frizzy hair, and the cheeky grin seemed to have everything going for him.

2013 Rory's 'annus horribilis'

We have just seen that for Henrik Stenson 2013 was a 'stellar' year. However, in stark contrast it was to be an 'annus horribilis' for Rory as he changed his equipment by signing a highly lucrative long term contract with Nike, he also changed his management company. He lost his focus and his form, he was swinging badly and clearly he rarely concentrated on golf and by November he admitted that 'I've seen more lawyers this year than I ever care to see again in my life'. On course he was nowhere near the player he'd become in the previous two years, and he also behaved particularly badly when he walked off the course midway through his second round at the Honda Classic in Florida in February when eleven, yes, that's 11, over par!!

However, Rory towards the end of the year had started on the Comeback Trail. This was shown by two important successes — one professional and one personal. His on course focus improved late in the year as he proved when he beat an in form Adam Scott on the first day of December to win the Australian Open by a single shot, and off course he proposed to his girlfriend in Sydney on the last day of 2013. Caroline said 'Yes', and Rory said goodbye to a year to forget. So in 2014 without a win on the European or American Tours for over a year Rory would definitely be on the CT.

2014 Rory's on the Comeback Trail

Because of their extra drive, determination and focus golfers often post a Comeback Trail win, and although that's exactly what Rory did in 2014 it came in the most unusual, unlikely and unexpected circumstances. After two seconds in the first two months, with recent form figures of 7-8-8-6 and his wedding invitations having been sent out, Rory was set to play in the European Tour's high profile BMW/PGA tournament at Wentworth in the penultimate week of May. However, on the eve of the tournament he had rung Caroline, his fiancée, to tell her that there would be no wedding and that their relationship was over. So at the pre-tournament press conference he was so visibly upset that golf punters believed that any chance Rory had of playing well let alone winning had gone. In fact the opposite happened and on Sunday with the leader Thomas Bjorn playing poorly, Rory came from off the pace with a superb final round 66 to win by one shot, and he was to win again within two months!

Rory's Glory

After taking a boating break with his mates Rory returned to play in the Scottish Open where after his usual bright start with an opening round of 64 he faded to finish T14th. The following week he was easy to back as 4th favourite at 20/1 for The Open and given his poor tournament record of just one top 20 in five pro starts and his second round 'Friday Blues' that was not surprising. Nevertheless at Hoylake he 'murdered' the par 5s and, leading from the start, the 25-year-old won his first Open Championship and with it the third leg of a Major Grand Slam.

He then went on to give a master class of long, straight driving as he won the WGC Bridgestone Invitational coming from off the pace to comfortably beat Sergio Garcia by two strokes. After that win the Irish superstar returned to golfing's Everest as he was ranked the World's No 1 golfer for the first time since March 2013. Then just seven days later in his first tournament as World No 1 he led from halfway and held off the challenge from Phil Mickelson to win the season's final major, the USPGA. So Rory's journey on the Comeback Trail was complete as he'd won back-to-back Majors and regained his place as the World's No 1 player.

Key elements in Rory's return to that No 1 spot

I think there were probably three crucial elements in the build up to Rory once again becoming the world's top ranked golfer.

First his fiancée's comments in April when she spoke of looking forward to having children may well have really brought home to Rory that he was not ready to 'settle down and face such responsibilities' and been the key to the telephone call that ended the relationship.

Second the sense of control he felt as a result of his decision to call off the marriage would have had a major positive effect as Rory must have felt that he had regained control of his life. If a person is troubled by an issue and feels that he/she is being swept along by the tide of events then they can find that making a decision to regain control of their lives can be extremely liberating. So Rory on his own admission soon became 'very single and very happy'.

The crucial third element was probably that having had the courage to make the decision to 'break-up' he felt mentally strong. That mental strength enabled him to 'live in the present' and so by focusing on the moment he avoided Mental Let Down and never became distracted by important victories, or talk of potential future achievements.

I suspect the catalyst for once again being able to have a deep focus on his golf was meeting Jack Nicklaus for lunch in May after which Rory surely realised that he had the talent to match the great man's records but would never do so if he allowed himself to be distracted and so a fully focused Rory — without any hint of Mental Let Down — went on to win the WGC Bridgestone and then the USPGA just a few weeks after winning The Open.

The simple fact was that Rory was another sportsman on the CT who had become a regular winner.

2013/14 Cricket: Mitchell Johnson — after injury, disciplinary and 'bottle' problems

Mitchell Johnson is an Australian left arm fast bowler who had had a period in the wilderness, a difficult recovery from a painful toe problem, so his form had been inconsistent. Indeed when playing in the 2011 Ashes series he'd been singled out by England's 'Barmy Army' because of his erratic bowling as they sang 'He bowls to the left, he bowls to the right, that Mitchell Johnson his bowling is shite'. He found that song so hard to take that he lost his 'bottle' on the field as it adversely affected his focus and concentration, and it was reported that he took mental skills advice on how to handle such criticism from an Aussie war veteran! Add in the fact that he was dropped earlier in 2013 for disciplinary reasons so when he was picked for the Ashes series starting in November it was clear that the mercurial Johnson was a player on the CT highly motivated both to prove himself to the home fans and especially to silence the Barmy Army whose criticism had stung him so much.

The rest as they say is history as his 90mph intimidating bowling brought him thirty seven wickets in the five match series in which he was Man of the Match in three of the five tests, the outstanding winner of the Man of the Series, and one of the key reasons why Australia 'whitewashed' England 5-0!

2014 Golf: JB Holmes — The Comeback Trail meets the God squad

You will remember JB from the God Squad chapter when he thanked his 'Lord and Saviour' after his first win in six years. The 32-year-old Kentuckian had been on the CT because back in 2011 he underwent serious brain surgery, and although he returned to the USPGA Tour without winning in 2012 he was again out of action a year later after a roller blading accident stopped him playing for five months. He was a two time winner who had been a star of the US-winning 2008 Ryder Cup team so he had a good golfing pedigree. Returning to play in 2014 his form steadily improved before he was the 66/1 winner of the Wells Fargo Championship in May by a single shot.

APPLYING THE COMEBACK TRAIL TO TEAMS

Although it is clearly easier to apply the CT to individuals than to teams there can be occasions when we can see a team is on the Comeback Trail.

There has been one recent outstanding example.

2013/14 Cricket: After three consecutive Ashes series defeats Australia were on the CT as they recorded a 5-0 whitewash win in the 2013/14 Ashes series

Aussie sportsmen are renowned for their fierce 'in your face' determination to win, their 'never say die ' attitude and as we saw in Chapter 7 on Inspiration by Comparison they feed off each other's successes. However, when England travelled to Australia for the Ashes Test series to be played in late 2013 and early 2014 the Aussies were not expected to win, England were the clear favourites as the recent record between the two countries clearly showed England were the better team.

- In the 2009 series in England — England regained the Ashes winning the series 2-1
- In the 2010/11 series in Australia — England retained the Ashes winning the series 3-1 — this was England's first win on Australian soil for 24 years.
- In the 2013 series in England — England again retained the Ashes winning the series 3-0.

So after three successive Ashes series defeats, and the humiliation in the last Ashes series on their own soil when England won three tests by an innings, and scored 500 or more runs in an innings four times in the series, Australia were most definitely on the Comeback Trail. From the first day of the first Test in Brisbane in late November to the final Test in Sydney in early January the Aussies dominated the series 'whitewashing' England 5-0 which had been on offer at 66/1!

It was clear from early in the series that this was an Aussie team with 'fire in its belly', with great team spirit, and in Mitchell Johnson, as we have just noted, they had a fast bowler who was himself on the CT. England, on the other hand, had all manner of problems and issues yet the simple fact was that here we had a wounded Australian team, with their spearhead bowler on the CT, playing on home soil showing all the extra determination, motivation and commitment you'd expect to see from a side on the Comeback Trail.

ASSESSING THE COMEBACK TRAIL

There can be little doubt that the CT has real legs as a predictive sporting tool as it enables us to identify individuals and possibly teams that have that extra motivation that can turn a good performance into a winning one, and as we have seen it can be applied to a range of sports. So I suggest that it is a good strategy to note all individuals and teams that are on the CT, and you may well find that some players on the CT list also are affected by other factors. Indeed five of our examples illustrate the point

- Luis Suarez — CT, The Nappy Factor, and use of a mental skills guru.
- JB Holmes — CT, and the God Squad.
- Danny Cipriani, Henrik Stenson, and Mitchell Johnson — CT, and use of a mental skills guru.

However, not every individual on the CT will be successful. For example, Irish golfer Padraig Harrington won The Open Championship in 2007 and 2008 and a third major when winning the 2008 PGA. However, the genial Irishman hasn't won on either the European or USPGA Tours since then, and although he is on the CT and had a narrow win in Thailand in early December 2014 he doesn't look like a 'winner about to happen' on the European or USPGA Tours especially as a new generation of fit, mentally tough and fearless young and long-hitting players have had such an impact on his sport, and so he wouldn't be a player I would expect to post a win on the two main tours any time soon. So a judgement call is clearly needed whenever a player is on the CT.

All of the factors we examine in this book are really useful sporting predictors yet they don't always apply to every sportsman. So there will be those who do not show improved form although they are on the CT. **Nevertheless the Comeback Trail is a very important powerful addition to our toolbox of factors that can increase sporting motivation**.

CHAPTER TEN
POSITIVE AND NEGATIVE MENTAL ASSOCIATIONS

You know yourself, when you return to your favourite bar, favourite restaurant, or favourite hotel you immediately feel comfortable and at ease. You feel assured, confident, and relaxed. Why? Because you have Positive Mental Associations [PMAs] with that bar, restaurant or hotel, all your links, experiences and associations with the place are completely positive so you are delighted to return. Your expectations are therefore also positive as you expect to enjoy yourself just as you had done on previous visits.

The same principle can apply to sportsmen who really can gain an advantage when they return to play at a venue, stadium, or course where they have had good previous experiences, because those PMAs enable them to feel comfortable, confident and relaxed. Without even consciously being aware of it those Positive Mental Associations can and do lead to positive performances so as there are very narrow margins between winning and losing any PMAs that lead to positive mental expectations can be the difference between success and failure and therefore can be a key factor that can enable a player to show improved and possibly winning form.

So let's start our journey down the PMA highway with NINE examples from THREE sports, Lawn tennis, Football, and Golf.

LAWN TENNIS
Pmas with Wimbledon SW19
Roger Federer without question is one of Tennis' all-time greats. His rise to mega stardom began when at Wimbledon in 1998 as a 16-year-old Roger first showed his huge potential winning both the boys singles final beating Irakli Labadze, and the boys' doubles partnered by Olivier Rochus. The young Federer fell in love with the place, he simply loved every aspect of Wimbledon as he enjoyed the grass surface, the unique atmosphere and the knowledgeable crowds. So with those strong Positive Mental Associations in place, and having won his only Junior Grand Slam title at Wimbledon it was virtually certain that the Swiss star would also secure his first Grand Slam win at Wimbledon and so it proved in 2003 when he beat Mark Philippoussis in what was to be the start of a tremendous run of success at SW19. The Swiss star went on to successfully defend his title in 2004 and 2005 beating American Andy Roddick each time.

Then a new adversary came on to the scene in the form of the charismatic young Spaniard Rafael Nadal who Federer beat in the 2006 and 2007 finals.

By that victory in 2007 Federer had won the Wimbledon singles title for five successive years so equalling the record of Bjorn Borg who had won in five consecutive years from 1976-1980 inclusive. So in 2008 when Federer again met Nadal in the Final he was aiming for an historic 6th consecutive win. However, in one of the best ever Wimbledon finals Federer narrowly lost by three sets to two with Nadal winning the final set 9-7!!

The Swiss superstar was to win Wimbledon again in 2009 when he beat Andy Roddick for the third time, and in 2012 when he beat Andy Murray he was winning the Wimbledon singles title for the 7th time a record matched only by Pete Sampras. So when he played Djokovic two years later in the 2014 final Federer was aiming to beat Sampras' record however, although it was one of the best ever finals, he lost by three sets to two.

Overall he has won 17 Grand Slam titles — Australian Open [4], French Open [1], US Open [5] — yet he won more of them at Wimbledon [7] than anywhere else.

There can be no doubt that the PMAs that started as a 16-year-old and were strengthened over the years played a considerable part in his amazing Wimbledon record.

FOOTBALL
PMAs with a former club and its stadium
Players who are progressing in their football careers are usually transferred to another bigger, richer and more successful club. So they will have many memories of their time at their former club where, in many cases, they made their name and so will often have a sense of gratitude to the staff and coaches who helped them develop. Indeed it may be that the transferred player is leaving the only professional club he has ever played for. Although individual cases vary we can usually be sure that if his new team play his former club he will have many **P**ositive **M**ental **A**ssociations because just the name of his former club will act as an inspiration, and if the match is at his former club's stadium then his PMAs will be even stronger.

Jordan Rhodes
Rhodes is a striker who while playing for Huddersfield had established a strong reputation as a goal scorer with 81 goals in 121 League and Cup games. That record of an average of 2 goals in every 3 games attracted plenty of interest from other clubs with the result that, in the summer of 2012, he was transferred from Huddersfield to Blackburn Rovers for £8 million. In the two seasons since his transfer he has played in both of Blackburn's away league games at Huddersfield's John Smiths' Stadium and on each occasion his PMAs with his former club and former Stadium were clearly evident as he scored in both games — in his first season he scored in the 2-2 draw, and in his second season he scored twice in his team's 4-2 away win. He has yet to play at his old ground in the current

2014/15 season as Blackburn's fixture at Huddersfield will be played on April 25th, the penultimate match of the regular season.

PMAS WHEN PLAYING AGAINST A PARTICULAR CLUB

Footballers don't have to be transferred to have PMAs as players tend to remember when they have played well on a particular ground, or against particular teams so when they play again against that team or on that ground those strong PMAs kick in [if you'll pardon the pun] and so they invariably play well.

Luis Suarez

Suarez is the world famous striker who had really strong PMAs when playing against Norwich City. So let's look at his record in his last five Premier League matches against the East Anglian club — they started on 28th April 2012 when he scored a hat-trick in a 3-0 win at Carrow Road and the following season with such strong PMAs he scored another hat-trick in September in a 5-2 win again in an away match at Carrow Road, and he followed up scoring a single goal in a 5-0 home win in January 2013.

So when Liverpool played Norwich at home in early Dec 2013 – guess what? — he didn't just get a hat-trick he actually went one better scoring four goals in a 5-1 Liverpool win. Finally in a crucial game at Norwich on Easter Sunday 20th April he scored again. In those five matches against Norwich he had scored three hat-tricks and 12, yes 12, goals, and he clearly loved playing away at Norwich's Carrow Road ground as he has scored 7 goals there, including two hat-tricks, in just three matches.

GOLF

With golf being the ultimate sport in which mental skills count we find there are countless examples over the years of players with really strong PMAs who nearly always play well on particular courses. American star golfer Phil Mickelson was definite when he said that 'when you come to a course where you have positive memories you play better'. Players can also have PMAs with particular countries, or in particular States in America or Australia and occasionally we see a player with Positive Mental Associations linked to a 'life event' such as a marriage. I have selected six examples.

PMAS WITH A LIFE EVENT

2013: Alex Cejka

Cejka is a Czech-born Golfer in his early forties who has 10 career wins although the last was in 2002. In 2012 he was married in Thailand so when Alex teed off on Thursday December 12th in the 2013 Thailand Open he was feeling really positive, really relaxed and really happy as it was 12 months to the day since he and his wife Alyssa had 'tied the knot' as it was their first wedding anniversary. He and his wife were together as they were to celebrate their anniversary by returning for a month's holiday to Phuket, the holiday island where they were married. So with such strong PMAs he was very relaxed, very calm, and very confident when he teed off. So it was no surprise that he shot a superb opening eight under par bogey free round of 64 to be the outright first round leader ahead of a strong field that included the eventual winner Sergio Garcia, Justin Rose, Henrik Stenson and Charl Schwartzel. Not surprisingly Cejka slipped down the leaderboard after his special 'anniversary' opening round finishing T18th.

PMAS WITH A SINGLE COURSE
2014: Stephen Gallacher
A golfer will certainly have **P**ositive **M**ental **A**ssociations when he returns to play in a tournament and on the course at which he posted his highest finish the previous year. On his return to that course he will recall the performance, the positive emotions, and so feel really confident knowing that having already played very well there he can play really well there again. Often therefore a player has his best finish in the same event and on the same course as he had the previous year. There have been many examples of this over the years however, the 39-year-old Scot Stephen Gallacher probably provided the best recent example with his record in the Dubai Desert Classic on the Emirates course where, after finishing 10th in 2010, he finished tied 2nd in his best finish of 2012, and then, in his first European Tour victory for nine years, he won at 70/1 in 2013 and then in 2014 at 45/1 he successfully defended his title. So in three successive years his best finish came on the Emirates course in Dubai in early February where his form figures now read 2-W-W, and you will recall that we have already examined his Dubai scorecards for 2013 and 2014 in the Chapter 8 on MLD and the Law of The Streaker.

1997: David Carter
In 1997 Carter was found unconscious in his hotel room two days before the Dubai Desert Classic and underwent emergency surgery as fluid was removed from his brain. Relaxed and knowing he had escaped death he returned to competitive golf five weeks later in the Cannes Open which was played on the short Royal Mougins course that placed a premium on accuracy so it was a course very well suited to David's game. Indeed the previous year, in 1996, he had shot a then course record nine under par 62 on his way to finishing second which was his best ever finish on the European Tour. So David had very potent **P**ositive **M**ental **A**ssociations with both the course and the tournament so no surprise that, although he hadn't played for five weeks, he finished tied 2nd after shooting another 62, this time in the final round.

PMAS WITH FAVOURITE COURSES
2013: Tiger Woods

Woods needs no introduction because until his back problems in 2014 he had dominated the world of golf since he burst on to the scene in 1997. However, he has become a classic example of a sportsman who feeds off PMAs as he showed conclusively in 2013 when he strengthened his position as the World's No 1 ranked player by winning five tournaments on the USPGA tour, and all five were on courses on which he'd previously won.

His five wins were in three 'ordinary' tournaments (shown with previous course wins and his winning margin in 2013):

	Previous wins	Won by
Farmers' Insurance Open at Torrey Pines	6	4
Arnold Palmer Invitational at Bay Hill	7	2
The Players Championship at Sawgrass	1	2

The other two were in World Golf Championship events

	Previous wins	Won by
WGC Cadillac at Doral	6	2
WGC Bridgestone at Firestone	7	7

So Tiger's five 2013 wins came on courses where he had collectively already posted 27 wins and he won them all by at least 2 shots!!

It is clear that, especially in recent years, Tiger has been at his best on courses on which he's previously been successful as they are courses to which he feels really strong PMAs and on which he therefore feels really comfortable, and very relaxed as he knows these courses suit his game as they 'fit his eye', he understands the greens, and the type and length of shots required at the key holes.

PMAS WITH A STATE AND A PARTICULAR COURSE
2007: Justin Leonard

Leonard is a Texan through and through. He was born in Dallas where he lives and went to the University of Texas so he has real PMAs when playing in his home state. This was particularly true of the LaCantera course in San Antonio which was the host course when Justin won the Texas Open for the first time in 2000, where he defended his title in 2001, and where he won it for the third time in 2007. That golf course suited Justin perfectly as it favoured players who were accurate ball strikers and were comfortable on the huge, tricky Bermuda grass greens. As one of his rivals Carl Paulson said 'this is a kind of second home to him as he feels really comfortable out there'. Comfortable, relaxed and happy playing in his home state on a course he knew how to play really well Justin had **P**ositive **M**ental **A**ssociations with both his beloved State and his favourite course.

PMAS WITH A PARTICULAR COUNTRY
1996: Guy Boros
Boros, the son of the two-time US Open golf champion Julius Boros, had never won in America until the penultimate weekend of August 1996 when there were two USPGA tournaments. The NEC World Series of Golf was held for the World's top players at the Firestone Course in Akron, Ohio while the other The Greater Vancouver Open was to be played in Vancouver, Canada. Guy, earlier in his career, had played for four years on the Canadian Tour winning the Atlantic Classic in 1989 and then two years later he won the Canadian Tour's Order of Merit in a successful year that included his second Canadian win in the British Columbian Open. So when Guy travelled to Vancouver although he was a 100/1 outsider he was in a really confident mood because he had strong **P**ositive **M**ental **A**ssociations with Canada based on those two wins and that Order of Merit success so he believed he could win there again. He did just that winning by one shot to give him his third win in Canada and his first on the USPGA Tour.

NEGATIVE MENTAL ASSOCIATIONS
When we started this Chapter I asked you to remember how you felt when you revisited a favourite bar, restaurant or hotel and how that led to positive mental associations and positive expectations. Well now let's put that process into reverse and think how you would feel if you had to revisit a bar, restaurant or hotel where you had a really poor, disappointing time when you had been there before. As a result of your experiences you would probably again expect poor service, poor food, and a poor overall experience. So let's put PMAs into reverse and see what happens when we have **N**egative **M**ental **A**ssociations.

Now before we go any further you will probably be saying to yourself that if I have bad experiences I would simply not return to the bar, restaurant or hotel and you'd be right you wouldn't, and neither would I. However, the golfer, tennis player, or footballer, indeed any professional sportsman, often has no choice as they have to play the same teams, or the same players, or the same opponents or return to the same stadiums, courses or tennis courts or to the same Major tournaments where they may have performed poorly, scored badly, lost their nerve, been injured or disciplined, or had the most outrageously bad luck. Usually they simply have no choice they have to return, and when they do they will suffer from powerful **N**egative **M**ental **A**ssociations.

So let's begin our journey down this new NMA pathway with three very interesting yet very different examples.

GOLF — NMAS BASED ON PREVIOUS DEFEATS
Greg Norman
The Aussie golfer who was nicknamed the 'Great White Shark', had two really upsetting experiences in Major golf Championships.

In 1987 in a play-off for the US Masters he lost to an outrageously lucky 140 foot chip-in by the American Larry Mize, and in 1990 in the Open at St. Andrews Greg shot a final round 76 and so was beaten by Nick Faldo who'd carded a 67! Those two horrendous experiences were to come back to haunt Greg years later at Augusta.

When Greg teed off in the 1996 US Masters he had a good record at Augusta. Although he had never won the tournament he had posted 7 top six finishes including 2nd twice, 3rd twice, 4th once, plus 5th and 6th place finishes. However, on Sunday April 14th 1996 it looked virtually certain that Greg would at last wear the famous Green Jacket that is presented to the winner of the US Masters as he had played superbly to build a six shot lead ahead of Nick Faldo going into that final day. The Aussie was the long odds on favourite at 1/7 with his nearest challenger Nick Faldo 10/1. However, slowly but surely the NMAs he felt after his defeats from winning positions by Mize in 1987 and crucially by Faldo in 1990 caught up with the 'Shark' so as he saw the ace stalker Faldo in his rear view mirror Greg's nerve cracked. At the end having started six ahead he was beaten by five strokes after he shot a six over par 78 compared to Faldo's brilliant 67. At the end Faldo was almost speechless when he shook Greg's hand he said, 'I don't know what to say ... I just want to give you a hug.' Those powerful **N**egative **M**ental **A**ssociations, one of which included Nick Faldo, had brought the 'Shark' another Augusta defeat ... and a hug!

FOOTBALL: NMAS BASED ON TIMING
Arsenal's early kick-off problems
Arsenal led the Barclays Premier League throughout the early months of the 2013/14 season. On 12th December they faced Manchester City, who were the bookies' favourite to win the title, so although early in the season this was definitely a big game, and it was given an early 12.45 pm Saturday kick off to enable it to be shown on the new BT Sport channel. Arsenal lost 6-3 and never looked as if 'they were in the match'. A one-off, a 'bad day at the office', were among the clichés that followed.

However, a similar result followed in another 12.45 pm kick off when Arsenal played Liverpool at Anfield on Saturday 8th February. The Gunners were amazingly 3-0 down after just 16 minutes as they couldn't resist Liverpool's early fast paced onslaught before they eventually lost 5-1.

Again the following month on 22nd March, in another Saturday early 12.45 pm kick off, Arsenal went to Stamford Bridge to play Chelsea, and again they were swept away early going 3-0 down after 17 minutes on their way to a 6-0 hammering!

Arsenal manager Arsene Wenger after that 6-0 defeat said that, 'It's puzzling. We were shocked and knocked down basically without feeling we had a chance.'

So Arsenal had played three key Saturday away games against the other three top teams going for the Premier League title, and all three ended in heavy defeats in which Wenger's team had conceded 17 goals!! Most interestingly after that third defeat at Chelsea the Arsenal captain and centre back Per Mertesacker said 'I don't know why, but it looks like we don't fancy early kick offs. It looks like we're going to have to apply to the FA to not play at 12.45.'

You can analyse those three results in a myriad of different ways but one thing seems clear. After that first heavy early Saturday kick-off defeat at the Etihad Arsenal took those NMAs forward to the next two big away early kick-off weekend games against their closest rivals and although Per Mertesacker was trying to make light of the situation by his comments he perhaps 'let the cat out of the bag' by pointing to the early kick-off times. NMAs ruled as Arsenal had developed an expectation that playing away against a top side in an early kick-off meant a heavy defeat. This was well illustrated the next and final time Arsenal faced another weekend early kick-off match away to one of their main Premier League rivals.

Fifteen days after their 6-0 thrashing at Stamford Bridge, the Gunners played on a Sunday with another early start in a 1.30 pm kick-off match at Goodison Park against Everton who were challenging Arsenal for that crucial fourth place in the Premier League which would bring Champions League football. Again, Arsenal never really made a game of it as Everton ran out comfortable 3-0 winners.

So overall in the four crucial early kick-off weekend away games against their closest rivals the Arsenal record was played 4, lost 4, goals for 4, goals against 20!!!!

GOLF: NMAS BASED ON DISLIKE OF A COURSE
Padraig Harrington

Harrington has 11 European Tournaments victories, two wins on the USPGA Tour as well as The Open championship in 2007 which he successfully defended in 2008. He also won the USPGA so he has three major wins, and the Dublin-born golfer was once as high as third in the World Rankings so let's be clear this jovial Irishman was a world class player.

Apart from the majors and the World Golf Championships the most prestigious and valuable tournament on the European Tour, is the Volvo PGA which is played annually in England in June at Wentworth. However, it's a tournament that Padraig has never enjoyed. Indeed he has stated openly and honestly that his game is not suited to the West Course at Wentworth and that he has sometimes played there solely from a sense of loyalty to the European Tour rather than from any expectation of success. So his tournament record is not surprisingly poor for a player of his undoubted class as his form figs of 13-60-11-56-17-45-MC in his first consecutive seven starts from 1996-2002 proved. Those strong early NMAs discouraged Padraig from playing so as a result he played just five times in the ten years from 2003 to 2012 although in that period he did post his first top tens in the tournament for the first time when sixth in both 2006 and 2010.

In the last two years however, it's been the same old story as he didn't play in 2013 and in 2014 he finished 61st!

Those strong early Negative Mental Associations prevented a proven world-class golfer from producing a single top five finish when playing in a very prestigious tournament on a course on which he's never felt comfortable.

ASSESSMENT

Positive Mental Associations were introduced in my very first golf annual published in 1994 and since then with the rapid growth in popularity of Positive Thinking we have seen a huge increase in sportsmen being encouraged to create as many and as strong a set of Positive Mental Associations as possible. In fact it's almost become compulsory after any defeat for a manager or coach to use the phrase 'let's take the positives out.' This, if done correctly, can of course be helpful, but it can also be very dangerous if its actual meaning becomes 'let's ignore the schoolboy mistakes, lack of concentration and poor decision making that led to our defeat.' Such an approach will not lead to improvement. If that is the attitude then the coach is misunderstanding the nature of positive thinking because improvement comes from a belief that virtually all aspects of sporting performance can be measured and analysed with specific tailor-made training programmes then created and developed. That is the positive path to improvement and certainly it doesn't come from the repetitive mantra stating that 'we must take the positives out.'

Although it takes time sports performance can be improved if a team or an individual can create a culture that emphasises a continuous positive mind-set that focuses on taking responsibility, seeing challenges as opportunities, and having clear objectives expressed in positive terms.

So let's return to those NMAs that Arsenal had on those away trips for early kick off matches against the other top clubs, and note that captain Per Mertesacker's comments were not those of a positive thinker as they didn't suggest that Arsenal's early kick off problem was soluble. Indeed his comments were literally irresponsible as they suggested that the solution to the problem lay with the FA for allowing early kick offs rather than with Arsenal's approach to those matches.

Negative Mental Associations can, of course, be reviewed, reframed, and reversed especially if a sportsman is working with a mental skills guru with whom he can discuss his feeling of failure and his negativity. There are, for example, techniques associated with NLP, Neuro Linguistic Programming, that can be used to reduce and eliminate bad memories, and with skilled help any experience can be reframed. So, for example, a golfer who misses the cut after 36 holes on a course he was playing competitively for the first time and has to go home without a pay cheque could say that he'll never play there again as the course doesn't suit him or he could decide to reframe his experience. Alternatively instead of mentally 'beating himself up' about his failure he could well realise that his scorecard was ruined by just four holes, one when he played an approach shot with the 'wrong' club, a second when because of course inexperience he misjudged the wind, and also when he twice lost concentration when missing two four-foot putts. So he can see that it was his errors that he can correct rather than the course that led to his poor result.

Overall when analysing any individual or team sporting event one question to be asked is what **P**ositive **M**ental Associations or **N**egative **M**ental **A**ssociations will follow for any of the individuals or teams involved?

INDEX